Truth and Truthmakers

Truths are determined not by w̶ world is. Or so realists about truth believe. ᴘʜᵢₗₒₛₒₚ theories correspondence theories of truth. Truthmaking theory, which now has many adherents among contemporary philosophers, is the most recent development of a realist theory of truth, and in this book D. M. Armstrong offers the first full-length study of this theory. He examines its applications to different sorts of truth, including contingent truths, modal truths, truths about the past and the future, and mathematical truths. In a clear, even-handed and non-technical discussion he makes a compelling case for truthmaking and its importance in philosophy. His book marks a significant contribution to the debate and will be of interest to a wide range of readers working in analytical philosophy.

D. M. ARMSTRONG's many publications include *A Materialist Theory of Mind* (1968) and *A World of States of Affairs* (1997).

CAMBRIDGE STUDIES IN PHILOSOPHY

General editors E. J. LOWE and WALTER SINNOTT-ARMSTRONG

Advisory editors
JONATHAN DANCY University of Reading
JOHN HALDANE University of St Andrews
GILBERT HARMAN Princeton University
FRANK JACKSON Australian National University
WILLIAM G. LYCAN University of North Carolina, Chapel Hill
SYDNEY SHOEMAKER Cornell University
JUDITH J. THOMSON Massachusetts Institute of Technology

Truth and Truthmakers

D. M. ARMSTRONG

Emeritus Professor of Philosophy, University of Sydney

CAMBRIDGE
UNIVERSITY PRESS

CAMBRIDGE UNIVERSITY PRESS
Cambridge, New York, Melbourne, Madrid, Cape Town, Singapore, São Paulo

Cambridge University Press
The Edinburgh Building, Cambridge CB2 8RU, UK

Published in the United States of America by Cambridge University Press, New York

www.cambridge.org
Information on this title: www.cambridge.org/9780521547239

First published 2004
Third printing 2007

Printed in the United Kingdom at the University Press, Cambridge

A catalogue record for this publication is available from the British Library

ISBN-13 978-0-521-83832-0 hardback
ISBN-13 978-0-521-54723-9 paperback

For Charlie Martin, who introduced me
to the notion of a truthmaker

Contents

Preface

My thoughts on truthmakers have only developed slowly. A brilliant shaft of light from Charlie Martin introduced me to the notion many years ago, but it took me a long time to understand the full implications of his idea. And only since 1997 have I put truthmaking itself at the centre of my work on metaphysics.

The concept of truthmaking has become widely diffused throughout the Australian philosophical community, and I am conscious of debts to John Bigelow, John Fox, Frank Jackson, George Molnar, Daniel Nolan, Greg Restall and probably others who have helped to create a climate of thought. In the meanwhile the same enterprise, and – rather wonderfully – the very same word, came to birth in the other hemisphere in a seminal 1984 article by Kevin Mulligan, Peter Simons and Barry Smith. Their subsequent work has since flowed together with the thinking that Martin taught, to the enrichment of us all. In England mention should be made of Hugh Mellor and his students. And in 2002 a conference on the topic of truthmakers was held in Manchester, one that I had the pleasure of attending. Martin returned to North America after some years at Adelaide and then Sydney, settling in the University of Calgary, from where his insistence on truthmakers had influence on a number of persons in the US and Canada, notably John Heil. I thank him for his help with this book. An American philosopher who uses the notion in his work but was not influenced by Martin is Herbert Hochberg. I thank him for valuable comment, especially on chapter 2.

Bertrand Russell in his later work spoke of the 'verifier', but was working with the notion of the truthmaker. He, I suppose, is the major ancestor of this powerful concept that is now available to the realist metaphysician, and is used by many of them.

A special issue of the periodical *Logique et Analyse*, edited by Peter Forrest and Drew Khlentzos and subtitled *Truth Maker and Its Variants*, has come to my notice at too late a point to take account of it. But it contains what seem to be a number of very useful contributions to truthmaker theory. It is to be noted that its asserted date of publication (2000) does not correspond to the date of its actual appearance. I would like to thank Angela Blackburn for her admirable copyediting.

Sydney 2003

1

An introduction to truthmakers

I first learnt to appreciate the power of the notion of a truthmaker from C. B. (Charlie) Martin. A survey of the arguments I was introduced to then should serve as a good introduction to this essay.

The time was the late 1950s, and Martin was a lecturer at the University of Adelaide. I was at Melbourne University. At the time we were both interested in the doctrine of phenomenalism, the claim that physical objects are constituted out of sense-data or sense-impressions. Neither of us had any sympathy for this view, but it was in the air at the time. The question for us was how it was best argued against.

Phenomenalists had a problem about physical objects and events at times that they are not being perceived. The solution to the problem generally given is to be found in embryo in Berkeley and became firm doctrine in John Stuart Mill. It involved an appeal to certain *counterfactual* truths. Counterfactual claims are often to be found in ordinary discourse, for instance, 'If you had not put your foot on the brake so promptly just then, there would have been a nasty accident.' There can be rational discussion of such claims, and it is plausible that they can be true as well as false, though some philosophers want to say that they are no more than 'assertible' or 'not assertible'. Perhaps, then, an account can be given of the physically unobserved in terms of what sort of perceptions would have been had if, contrary to fact, a suitable perceiver had actually perceived them. In Mill's striking phrase, a physical object becomes a mere 'permanent possibility of sensation'.

Many *prima facie* difficulties for this line of defence using counterfactuals were known. But Martin asked a simple question that seemed to go to the heart of the problem. Suppose that the required counterfactual propositions are indeed true. What are the truthmakers for these truths? Must there not be *some way that the world is* in virtue of which these truths are true? *What is it?* How does the world make these truths true?

Realists about the physical world will have no difficulty in answering Martin's question. Berkeley had an answer, even if an obscure and difficult

1

answer, in the *archetype* of the world that he supposed to exist in the eternal mind of God. A realist about unfulfilled possibilities might have an answer. But what answer had the actual phenomenalists got? All these philosophers had available for truthmakers were the *actual* sense-data or sense-impressions had by actual minds. Truthmakers for true counterfactuals about the perception of unobserved material reality would therefore have to be found in the actual, bitty, sense-data. As a result, unobserved physical reality cannot, for the phenomenalist, be what we all think it is in our unphilosophical moments: something ontologically *additional* to observed physical reality.

A bad enough result, one would think. But worse follows. Consider a physical world without any minds in it. That seems to be a possibility, indeed in view of the delicacy of the initial conditions under which life evolved, it seems to be a physical possibility, one compatible with the actual laws of nature. What can the phenomenalist say about such a world? Every physical truth about individual objects and processes must be given a counterfactual analysis in terms of perceptions not actually had. But what truthmakers in that sort of world will there be for these truths? None, it would seem. Such a world is empty of perceptions and the minds that have these perceptions, therefore it is empty, period. So for a phenomenalist there cannot be a physical world empty of minds.

I do not want to claim that these arguments are *absolutely conclusive* against phenomenalism. I deny that there are such arguments in metaphysics, and arguments using truthmakers are no exception. In the present case, for instance, a Berkeleyan idealist, such as the contemporary Oxford idealists John Foster and Howard Robinson, might even welcome them. But I claim that truthmaker arguments are very powerful, that, in Mill's phrase, they are considerations capable of influencing the intellect. Their power in the critique of phenomenalism is, I trust, obvious.

Let us turn from phenomenalism to Gilbert Ryle's account of the mind. As is well known, Ryle bolstered his quasi-behaviouristic account of mental states, events and processes in *The Concept of Mind* (1949) by continual reference to *dispositions*. Certain mental states, in particular beliefs, he saw as fundamentally dispositional. It is a mark of dispositions that they need not be manifested, perhaps at any time during the existence of the thing that has the disposition, although, of course, the physical possibility of that manifestation is involved in the very notion of a disposition. The brittle thing may never break; the elastic thing need never be first stretched and then allowed to return to its previous unstretched state. Similarly, a person might hold a belief, but never manifest that belief in behaviour during the whole of a life. No problem, then, for the Rylean account of mind. Unmanifested beliefs are no more than a particularly sophisticated sort of unmanifested disposition.

So, I think, Ryle saw it. But he could only so see the matter because he was working in a philosophical climate that saw little need to take up metaphysical (ontological) questions, and in particular no need to consider the question of the truthmaker for dispositional truths about minds. I think he was quite right to claim an essential role for dispositionality in the elucidation of our notion of the mental. That was a great and lasting contribution. But we need then to go on to consider the question of the truthmaker for these dispositional truths. What is there in the world in virtue of which these truths are true? Ryle had no answer.

Once we do raise the truthmaker question, then our view of the nature of mind will very likely be transformed and we will move in a quite un-Rylean direction. We will (very likely) identify a belief, say, with some inner *state* of the mind (materialist metaphysicians will identify it further with some state of the brain) that, in suitable circumstances, but only in suitable circumstances, will manifest itself in various ways, some of which ways may be outward behaviour.

Of course, even if under the influence of the truthmaker question we do 'move inside' to the brain (or the soul), there will be plenty of room for disagreement about the exact nature of the inner state that should be postulated. For myself, I incline to a *categorical* state, a state involving non-dispositional properties, and, as I now understand the matter, a state that requires to be supplemented by the relevant laws of nature. (The laws of nature, in turn, cannot be mere truths, but must be conceived ontologically.) Martin thought of the state required as having a categorical 'side' but as also involving *powers*, powers that are not reducible to the categorical, and which serve as his substitute for laws of nature. Others take subtly different views. But the truthmaker insight, as I take it to be, prevents the metaphysician from letting dispositions 'hang on air' as they do in Ryle's philosophy of mind. That is the ultimate sin in metaphysics, or at any rate, in a realist metaphysics.

2

The general theory of truthmaking

We have noticed already that simply to accept the idea that truths have truthmakers by no means dictates just what these truthmakers are. The question what truthmakers are needed for particular truths (what we take to be truths!) can be, and regularly is, as difficult as the question of metaphysics, the question of ontology. To ask the truthmaker question is, I maintain, a promising way to regiment metaphysical enquiry. But it is not a royal road. No such roads are available in philosophy. In this work I will defend various particular answers to the truthmaker question, sometimes (but not invariably) defending metaphysical positions that I have advocated in earlier work, but here always putting the truthmaking question at the centre. All the more reason then, to distinguish between the general theory of truthmaking and particular answers that may be given to truthmaking questions. The division is not all that sharp. There is, very properly, interaction between one's general theory of truthmaking and the particular truthmakers one postulates for particular classes of truths. The two enterprises have to be brought into reflective equilibrium. But it does seem worthwhile to make the distinction, and this chapter will be given over to the general theory with only glances at particular doctrines.

The notion of the truthmaker may be traced right back to Aristotle. (See, in particular, *Categories*, 14b, 14–22.) Aristotle's remarks were noted by a number of leading Scholastic philosophers, but the notion seems after this to have gone underground for some centuries, although intimations of it may be found here and there. The notion is present in Russell's thought, and in his later philosophizing he introduced a term for the notion, the somewhat unfortunate word 'verifier' (Russell, 1940, 1948, 1959).[1] Reference to truthmakers, and some development of truthmaking theory, is now quite widespread among philosophers working in Australia. I think that the source is always C. B. Martin, as certainly it was for me. But the very same notion, and the very same term, were introduced quite independently by Kevin Mulligan, Peter Simons and Barry Smith in a joint article 'Truth-makers' published in 1984. They provide a suggestive quotation from Husserl, and mention Russell and the *Tractatus* by Wittgenstein.

2.3. THE TRUTHMAKING RELATION

The idea of a truthmaker for a particular truth, then, is just some existent, some portion of reality, in virtue of which that truth is true. The relation, I think, is a cross-categorial one, one term being an entity or entities in the world, the other being a truth.[2] (I hold that truths are true *propositions*, but will leave this matter aside until 2.6.) To demand truthmakers for particular truths is to accept a *realist* theory for these truths. There is something that exists in reality, independent of the proposition in question, which makes the truth true. The 'making' here is, of course, not the causal sense of 'making'. The best formulation of what this making is seems to be given by the phrase 'in virtue of'. It is in virtue of that independent reality that the proposition is true. What makes the proposition a truth is how it stands to this reality.

Two questions immediately arise. First, do truthmakers actually *necessitate* their truths, or is the relation weaker than that, at least in some cases? Second, do *all* truths have truthmakers, or are there some areas of truth that are truthmaker-free, modal truths for instance? My answers to these questions are, first, that the relation is necessitation, absolute necessitation, and, second, that every truth has a truthmaker. I will call these positions respectively Truthmaker Necessitarianism and Truthmaker Maximalism.

Turning first to Necessitarianism, the first thing to notice is that the necessitation cannot be any form of entailment. Both terms of an entailment

---

[1] I am indebted to the late George Molnar for pointing this out to me. Russell's later work has been amazingly neglected. Herbert Hochberg has further pointed out to me that as early as 1921, in the *Analysis of Mind*, p. 277, Russell uses the word 'verified' where he means 'made true by'.

[2] Ken Barber has asked whether there are any other cases of cross-categorial relations. One could say 'yes, the relation of difference', but that is rather trivial. Whether there are other important cross-categorial relations, I do not know. It will prove to be important later that the relation is an *internal* one.

relation must be propositions, but the truthmaking term of the truthmaking relation is a portion of reality, and, in general at least, portions of reality are not propositions. The simplest of all truthmaking relations is that which holds between any truthmaker, T, which is something in the world, and the proposition <T exists>.[3] Here, clearly, the relation has to be cross-categorial.

It might be said, instead, that in this simple case the relation holds between *T's existence* and the proposition <T exists>. Presumably, *T's existence* is here supposed to be a state of affairs. I think, however, that it is a mistake to recognize states of affairs having this form. To do so seems to turn existence into a *property* of T. Although 'exists' is a perfectly good predicate, I think with Kant that it is a mistake to recognize an ontological property of existence. But if the Kantian position is wrong, *T's existence* would still be something in the world, and so the relation between it and the proposition <T exists> would still be a cross-categorial one.

This very simple relation between T and <T exists> may be thought to be rather trivial. Would it not be sufficient for the purposes of truthmaking theory to *start* in each case from truths having the form <T exists> and then spell out truthmaking relations in terms of entailments of propositions of this sort? The difficulty with this suggestion is that the truthmaking relation seems to hold in cases where entailment is completely lacking. Suppose that it is true that there exists a certain quantity of water in a certain place at a certain time. Will not a sufficiently dense conglomeration of H_2O molecules in that space at that time be a truthmaker for this truth? It seems to me that we ought to accept such truthmakers. But if we replace this truthmaker, as we can do easily enough, with a truth of existence, this truth does not *entail* the first truth. For entailment we need an additional premise: that a quantity of water is a certain sort of conglomeration of H_2O molecules. But how is a truthmaker for this additional premise to be spelled out in terms of entailments? So I say that the conglomeration of H_2O molecules at a certain place and time (the truthmaker) necessitates that <there is water at that place and time> (the truth), but this is not entailment.

But what is the argument for saying that a truthmaker must necessitate a truth it is truthmaker for? Here is an argument by *reductio*. Suppose that a

---

[3] I will use < . . . > to pick out propositions, a device I was introduced to by Paul Horwich, but regularly will not bother about this in simple cases, e.g. proposition *p*. These angle brackets may be iterated for propositions about propositions.

suggested truthmaker T for a certain truth p fails to necessitate that truth. There will then be at least the possibility that T should exist and yet the proposition p not be true. This strongly suggests that there ought to be some further condition that must be satisfied in order for p to be true. This condition must either be the existence of a further entity, U, or a further truth, q. In the first of these cases, T + U would appear to be the true and necessitating truthmaker for p. (If U does not necessitate, then the same question raised about T can be raised again about U.) In the second case, q either has a truthmaker, V, or it does not. Given that q has a truthmaker, then the T + U case is reproduced. Suppose q lacks a truthmaker, then there are truths without truthmakers. The truth q will 'hang' ontologically in the same sort of way that Ryle left dispositional truths hanging (Ryle, 1949).

Perhaps this argument gives sufficient support to Truthmaker Necessitarianism. But someone who accepted Necessitarianism for truthmakers might still hold that there can be truths that lack necessitation by a truthmaker. May there not be truths – such as q in the previous paragraph – that lack any truthmaker? Maximalism is needed to rule this out. What, then, is my argument for Maximalism?

I do not have any direct argument. My hope is that philosophers of realist inclinations will be immediately attracted to the idea that a truth, any truth, should depend for its truth for something 'outside' it, in virtue of which it is true. What I then offer in this essay is a running through of the main categories of truths, suggesting what I hope are reasonably plausible truthmakers in each category. I do not expect that my suggestions will all be accepted! Different metaphysicians, different proposed truthmakers. But I hope enough will be done to show that there are real prospects of providing truthmakers in all cases, and that this will encourage realists to take a favourable attitude to Maximalism. So let us treat Maximalism as a hypothesis to be tested by this whole work.

2.3.1. Supervenience

I have so far explicated truthmaker theory in terms of individual truthmakers for individual truths (although, as we shall see, there is no question of a one-one correlation of truthmakers and truths). But perhaps this piecemeal procedure can be bypassed. John Bigelow has introduced the very attractive slogan 'Truth supervenes on being' (1988, ch. 19). It looks rather good. Given all that there is, is one not given all truth? Truth ought to be determined by being, and that by an absolute necessity. In particular, if anything that is true had not been true, then being would have to have been different in some way.

It would seem incidentally that not only does truth supervene on being, but being supervenes on truth. For if anything that has being did not have being, then something that is true would not be true. The supervenience is symmetrical. (The word 'supervenience' suggests an asymmetry, but there seems nothing in the concept to rule out symmetry.) We will come back to this matter in the next section.

The first thing to be said here in criticism of Bigelow's suggestion is that if this is to be the sole explication of the truthmaking relation, then it will rule out any serious attribution of truthmakers for modal truths, in particular for necessary truths. Suppose, or try to suppose, that some necessary truth, say $<2 + 2 = 4>$, is not true. How would being differ? There seems to be no coherent answer. It is true of course that many sympathizers with a truthmaking programme have thought that nothing but trivial truthmakers *can* be given for modal truths. But in accordance with Maximalism, I will be attempting to do better than that in this work.

With respect to contingent truths, Bigelow's slogan seems true and valuable, and perhaps he intended no more. But to remain with it as the sole insight needed for contingent truths would still be unfortunate. It takes focus away from the piecemeal task of finding plausible truthmakers for important classes of truths, a task that ought to be undertaken by realist metaphysicians. Consider, for instance, the difficult case – difficult for truthmaking theory – of contingent but universally quantified truths (with existence of the subject term presupposed). The truth $<$all electrons have charge $e>$ may do as an example. Suppose that there are electrons, but that, contrary to the truth, some of these electrons lack charge e. (Perhaps the charge on these electrons is just a little bit smaller.) It is obvious that *being* would then have to be different. Supervenience holds. This, though, is not all that needs be said about truths of this sort. At least if we are Maximalists, we need to enquire just what are the particular truthmakers for these truths.[4]

---

[4] Bigelow's own position about these sorts of truth is that what we have is an *absence of falsemakers*. But since he rejects *absences* from his ontology, I think that here he does not advance beyond the supervenience thesis.

2.3.2. *Expressibility*

I have suggested that the converse of the Bigelow thesis holds, at least for contingent truths. If anything had been different in any way from what there actually is, the totality of the body of truths would have had to be different in some way. But it needs to be noted that this is a further, and perhaps disputable, thesis. It is the thesis that Stephen Read (2000, pp. 68–9) calls *Expressibility*. For all being, there is a proposition (perhaps one never formulated by any mind at any time) that truly renders the existence and nature of this being. When Wittgenstein said 'Whereof one cannot speak, thereof one must be silent' he was (perhaps) suggesting that there were existences, or aspects of existence, that of necessity could not give rise to truths. At any rate, it seems that such a thesis can be held. A presumably different way in which expressibility might fail is if there could not be infinite propositions (presumably only available, on the supposition that there are such things, to infinite minds), yet there was infinity in the world. I will leave consideration of Expressibility at this point. I have a rationalist prejudice in its favour, but no particular arguments to offer for this prejudice.

2.3.3. *Truthmaking an internal relation*

It should be noted that if, as argued, the truthmaking relation is a necessitating relation, then it is an internal relation. I mean by calling a relation internal that, given just the terms of the relation, the relation between them is necessitated. Given the terms 7 and 5, in that order, then the relation of *greater in number than* must hold between them. In the same way, given a certain real object, and a certain proposition, in that order, then the truthmaking relation (or the falsemaking relation) is automatically determined, fixed, necessitated. And although the matter requires further discussion at a later point, I suggest it is an attractive ontological hypothesis that such a relation is no addition of being. Given just the terms, we are given the ontology of the situation. The relation is not something over and above its terms (which is *not* to say that the relation does not hold, *not* to say that it does not exist).

2.4. FALSEMAKERS

Philosophers who are introduced to the concept of a truthmaker quickly notice that there is room for the concept of a falsemaker. It is the notion of a pair, some entity in the world and a proposition, such that the entity necessitates that the proposition is false. But although the notion seems a perfectly legitimate one, for a long time I could see no great use for it. Every truthmaker for a truth *p*, it would seem, is a falsemaker for the proposition <not-*p*>. And if something is a falsemaker for *p*, then again it is a truthmaker for the contradictory of *p*. But do we need to give much attention to the notion of a falsemaker?

However, falsemakers do play a more useful, or at any rate more interesting, role in some cases. Consider, in particular, one sub-class of modal truths: truths of impossibility. Suppose it is true that <it is impossible that *p* and not-*p* be both true> but necessary that one of the conjuncts be true. The truthmakers for the true conjunct will *simultaneously* be falsemakers for the other conjunct. (See further 8.8.)

Again, consider the truth that a certain wall is painted green. It seems reasonable to suppose that greenness is some sort of positive property (given what we know about colour, perhaps not an ontologically high-class property, not a 'sparse' one in David Lewis's terminology), and the wall's having that property is the truthmaker for that truth. Consider now the further truths that the wall is not white, is not red, is not . . . One may suggest that the wall makes these truths true by being a falsemaker for the corresponding positive attributions of colour. This in turn may encourage the idea that it is not necessary to postulate negative truthmakers for negative truths. Here we have the interesting, even if as I think ultimately unsatisfactory, 'Incompatibility theory' of truthmakers for negative truths.[5] (See 5.2.1 for discussion of this theory.)

2.5. THE ENTAILMENT PRINCIPLE

We come to what will prove a very important thesis in truthmaking theory. Suppose that T is a truthmaker for proposition *p*. Suppose further that *p* entails proposition *q*, with the exact force here of 'entails' subject to discussion. Then T will be truthmaker for *q*. This may be informally symbolized:

$$T \rightarrow p$$
$$\underline{p \text{ entails}^* q}$$
$$\therefore T \rightarrow q$$

[5] The link between Incompatibility theories and falsemaking was brought to my attention by Peter Simons.

The arrow is the truthmaking relation, a non-propositional necessity I have argued. The star symbol indicates that if this principle is to be applied in full generality, then the entailment here cannot be classical entailment. The problem with using classical entailment from my point of view is that if p is a contingent truth, then, since a contingent truth classically entails all necessary truths, any such truth can be substituted for q, thus making any contingent truth a truthmaker for any necessary truth. This robs truthmaking theory of all interest for the case of necessary truths. Some truthmaker theorists may accept this conclusion – it accords with Wittgenstein's view of necessary truths in the *Tractatus* – but I am hoping to provide *relevant* truthmakers for all truths.

The exact limitations to be placed on entailment in the suggested Entailment principle is a technical matter, one that I am not equipped to discuss. Suggestions have been made by Restall (1996) and Read (2000), and I will simply assume that something is available. I am not arguing that classical entailment should be abandoned, but am urging that a connective that does not allow the distressing explosion of truthmakers for necessary truths should be used in this particular context. Horses for courses.

We may note, however, another strategy of some interest. This is to accept classical entailment, but to narrow the scope of the Entailment principle in some way. Restall reports (1996, sec. II) that one such suggestion was made by Frank Jackson. Jackson suggested that the values substituted for p and q should be restricted to contingent truths. To this Contingency restriction, as we may call it, Restall objects that, given classical entailment, contingent truth p entails $<p$ & $N>$, where N is any necessary truth. But $<p$ & $N>$ is a *contingent* truth. So, given the Entailment principle, any truthmaker for p is the truthmaker for $<p$ & $N>$. But it is a very plausible proposition of truthmaking theory that a truthmaker for a conjunction is a truthmaker for each conjunct. So, again, the truthmaker for p is a truthmaker for N. Hence the Contingency restriction fails.

It seems to me that Jackson's suggestion can still be upheld provided we make a further restriction, which may be called the restriction to *purely* contingent truths. A purely contingent truth is one that does not contain a necessary conjunct. Nor, to ward off further cases suggested to me by Glenn Ross, whom I thank for discussion here, does it contain any necessary truth as a component in a conjunction (or disjunction or whatever) at any level of analysis. A purely contingent truth is one that is contingent *through and through*. Given such a restriction the Entailment principle seems to hold, and to be useful in truthmaking theory, even if the entailment is classical. In any case, it may be noted that 'impure' contingent truths of the sort that Restall points to are not ones that truthmaking theory has much occasion to work with.

An important point to keep in mind about the Entailment principle is that even where T is a *minimal* truthmaker for the entailing proposition *p* it will not necessarily be a minimal truthmaker for the entailed *q*. The fairly straightforward notion of a minimal truthmaker will be discussed in 2.10.

2.6. TRUTHS AND FALSEHOODS ARE PROPOSITIONS

Truthmaker theorists have so far paid little attention to the other term of the relation: the truths that truthmakers make true. What are the *truthbearers*, the bearers of the predicates 'true', 'not true' and 'false'? In his very useful book *Theories of Truth* Richard Kirkham argues for a tolerant attitude (1992, 2.4). He assembles evidence that different philosophers have taken very different entities to be truthbearers:

Among the candidates are beliefs, propositions, judgments, assertions, statements, theories, remarks, ideas, acts of thought, utterances, sentence tokens, sentence types, sentences (unspecified), and speech acts. (p. 54)

This should give us all pause. I nevertheless (now!) wish to say that it is *propositions* that constitute the central case for a theory of truthbearers. We can certainly apply the truth predicates very widely, but I am inclined to think that all other suggested truthbearers besides propositions are called truthbearers on account of their relationship to certain propositions. At any rate, I am going to begin from the assumption that truths are (centrally) true propositions, and falsehoods are (centrally) false propositions. But what are propositions? What is their ontological status?

There are metaphysicians who are prepared to postulate a realm of propositions over and above the space-time world. But, presumably, we could not stand in any causal or nomic relation to such a realm. And if we cannot stand in such relations to propositions it is unclear that such a postulation is of any explanatory value. At any rate, as a naturalist, I want to look for a this-worldly account of propositions.

One view that I wish to reject is that propositions that are linguistically expressed can be identified with equivalence classes of synonymous sentences (contrary to what I said in my 1997, 10.3.1). Synonymy depends on meaning, not meaning on synonymy. Here I am taught by Marian David. He has pointed out to me that it is possible that a particular equivalence class of synonymous sentence (or word) tokens could, while remaining a synonymous class, have had a different meaning from the one it actually has. To make this vivid, consider that same class of tokens 'in another possible world'. Suppose that in this other world the word 'cat' is our word for a dog. The class of tokens of 'cat' in that world is still an equivalence class under the relation of synonymy. Yet those tokens in that other world pick out dogs, not cats. So, although it may be useful at times to consider such equivalence classes, it is the meaning that each individual token has that provides the semantic unity of the class.

Leaving this error behind, I begin with a suggestion that will require to be modified before being satisfactory. This preliminary suggestion is that propositions are the *intentional objects* of beliefs and certain thoughts. That is on the mental side. On the linguistic side they are the intentional objects of statements. I do not want to read too much metaphysics into the phrase 'intentional objects'. Beliefs are essentially beliefs *that* something is the case. Whatever is believed to be the case may then be said to be 'the intentional object of that belief', using this as a technical term only. And that is a proposition. Some thoughts that are not beliefs, mere suppositions and idle fancies for instance, also have as their intentional object that something is the case, and these objects are again propositions. Meaningful statements are statements that something is the case, and what is meant may be said to be 'the intentional object of the statement'. These objects, too, are propositions. (I will here ignore the very important distinction, and any complications that come with that distinction, between speaker's meaning and conventional meaning. I also ignore any complications introduced by indexicals.)

Propositions, on this view, are abstractions, but not in any other-worldly sense of 'abstraction', from beliefs, statements and so on. They are the *content* of the belief, what makes the belief the particular belief that it is; or else the *meaning* of the statement, what makes the statement the particular statement that it is. That the content or meaning is an abstraction becomes clear when we notice that contents and meanings are types rather than tokens. Beliefs in different minds may have the very same content, numerically different statements may have the very same meaning. Content and meaning seem to be properties, though they are doubtless not purely intrinsic (non-relational) properties, of token beliefs and token statements. Furthermore, these properties will, in turn, very often be *impure* properties, in the sense that they are properties that involve essential reference to particulars, such as the property *being descended from Charlemagne*.

To go further than this here would take us, inappropriately, deep into the philosophy of mind and the philosophy of language. I would be hoping for a naturalistic theory of content and meaning, and so a naturalistic theory of the identity conditions for propositions. Our beliefs, statements and so on have certain intentional objects. There are, of course, desperately difficult problems concerning intentionality – in particular the problem how we can think and say what is not true – and some philosophers think that these problems should be addressed by metaphysics, by ontology. My own view is that these are problems, horribly difficult problems to be sure, to be addressed within the philosophy of mind, or perhaps its successor: cognitive science. But here I will simply assume that there is intentionality in the realm of the mental and, when the use of language is informed by mentality, in the linguistic realm. Indeed, I would wish to uphold a representational account of the mental. Every mental state, process and event has, or is linked to, some representational content. (This includes perception, it includes bodily sensation, which I take to be bodily perception, and it also includes introspective awareness.) If this is right, the mind is a purely intentional system. Of course, only some of these contents are contents that admit the predicates 'true' or 'not true'. Desires have content, but are neither 'true' nor 'not true'. (I think that perceptions do admit of these predicates, although it is customary among philosophers to speak more guardedly of 'veridical' and 'non-veridical' perceptions.)

We should, however, note that what follows the 'that', and so is a proposition, may not only be false but an impossibility. There is a proposition <there is a counter-instance to Fermat's last theorem>, although we now know that there can be no such counter-instance. Hobbes believed that the circle could be squared, though this is an impossibility. That <the circle can be squared> was surely the intentional object of his belief. This suggests, by the way, that an analysis of intentionality in terms of possible worlds will not succeed.

It may also be noted that an account of propositions as intentional objects (one sort of intentional object – the sort that can be true or false) will have to allow for vagueness in many propositions. Intentional objects of actual thoughts and statements can be very vague, even if there is no vagueness in reality, as I should like to think. And very vague beliefs and statements can still have truthmakers. But as one who has done no work on the topic of vagueness I will not investigate further this corner of truthmaking theory. It may be hoped that nothing of first importance will be thereby omitted.

But at this point we must recognize that the account given of true propositions, in particular, is somewhat unsatisfactory. We have attached propositions to beliefs, statements and so on. Cannot there be truths which nobody has or will believe, or even formulate, much less state? Consider Newton and his image of the ocean of undiscovered truth that he said lay before him, reaching far beyond his own discoveries. We understand this well enough, and would continue to understand it even in the absence of an all-knowing creator or the ocean of truth yielding up all its secrets in the future. We may call such truths unexpressed truths. Generalizing to include falsehoods, we can speak of 'unexpressed propositions'.

True unexpressed propositions will be truths without any *concrete* truth-bearers. Some philosophers may think that we can ignore such cases. But in fact I think that this would be a mistake. They are, for me at least, conceptually very important. The reason for this is that the concept of such truths is needed to make sense of Truthmaker Necessitarianism. How can truthmakers necessitate truthbearers if the truthbearers are beliefs, statements and so on? How can something in the world, say the state of affairs of the dog's being on the dog-bed, *necessitate* that I have a belief that this is the case, or that somebody states that it is the case? What is necessitated can be no more than the true *proposition* <the dog is on the dog-bed>. That is why propositions must be the true truthbearers, or at any rate the most fundamental truthbearers.

This in turn requires that we now modify the suggested account of propositions as intentional objects. Actual intentional objects require actual beliefs, actual statements and suchlike, and the world cannot necessitate such actualities. So we need an account of propositions that abstracts from whether or not they are expressed.

We can, I believe, cover the cases of unexpressed propositions by treating them as possibilities, mere possibilities, of believing, or contemplating, or linguistically expressing the unexpressed proposition. If we think of the intentional object of an expressed proposition as some (hard to analyse) *property* of its vehicle, then unexpressed propositions will be *uninstantiated* properties. But I would wish to exclude uninstantiated properties from my ontology. Properties of things are, I think, *ways* that things are, and the notion of a way that nothing is seems ontologically near unintelligible. I would find an account of unexpressed propositions in terms of uninstantiated properties acceptable only if a deflationary account of these uninstantiated properties is given. We can do this deflation, I hope, by equating these uninstantiated properties with the *mere possibility* of the instantiation of such a property. It will then be necessary, of course, to consider what are the truthmakers for these truths of mere possibility. That task must here be postponed until we reach the whole great question of truthmakers for modal truths in chapters 7 and 8. We shall find, I believe, that this-worldly truthmakers for truths of mere possibility are not all that hard to find.

Truthmakers for truths necessitate, absolutely necessitate, those truths, or so I have argued. It seems clear, however, that truthmakers cannot necessitate actual beliefs, thoughts and statements. So propositions taken as *possible* intentional objects are the only things that truthmakers can actually *necessitate*.

2.7. CONNECTING TRUTH WITH REALITY

Propositions correspond or fail to correspond to reality. If what has been said about propositions in the previous section is correct, then it becomes pretty clear that the correspondence theory of truth can and should be upheld. Truth is a matter of the intentional object of an actual or possible belief, actual or possible statement, and so on, corresponding with some real object. (In both cases, of course, 'object' is to be taken in a broad way.)[6] What has been the bane of the correspondence theory, at least in recent philosophy, is the idea that the correspondence between true propositions and the reality in virtue of which they are true is a one-one correspondence. In the minimalist theory of truth, in the form put forward by Paul Horwich (1990), the theory of truth is confined to a simple (and true) principle, the equivalence schema: $<p$ is true$>$ if and only if p. If, under the influence of the one-one correspondence view, a correspondence theory is accepted, then we get a quite similar but metaphysically very extravagant theory: p is true if and only if it corresponds to the *fact* or *state of affairs* that p. Faced with a forced choice between the Horwich theory and this one-one correspondence theory, I would opt for Horwich's view.

But there is a middle way, better than either Horwich's actual view or the metaphysical version of his theory. We can accept a correspondence theory, but in a form where it is recognized that the relation between true propositions and their correspondents is regularly many-many. Indeed, even if we restrict ourselves to *minimal* truthmakers, I do not think that we ever get a one-one case. The correspondents in the world in virtue

---

[6] '[D]eflationists do not connect truth with reality in the way that traditional correspondence theorists hope to do': Williams, 2002, p. 150.

of which true propositions are true are our truthmakers. One thing that should recommend this more nuanced approach is the now widespread recognition that, in the theory of *properties*, it is in general a mistake to look for a one-one correlation to hold between properties and predicates. The extra space that this gives one can be used, for instance, to articulate a theory of what David Lewis called the *sparse* properties, the ones which he (and I) hold to be the ontologically significant properties of objects, those in terms of which the world's work is done. And indeed, the complex relations that predicates stand in to properties can quite naturally be thought of as part of truthmaker theory. Of course, there are philosophers who deny that we should recognize properties in our ontology. But the next chapter will argue that there is a strong case in truthmaking theory for accepting the existence of properties that are independent of the mere true application of predicates.

2.8. A REALIST DEFINITION OF TRUTH?

We will work, then, with the following theory of the nature of truth:

p (a proposition) is true if and only if there exists a T (some entity in the world) such that T necessitates that p and p is true in virtue of T.

We note that the 'only if' is particularly controversial even among those who accept some form of truthmaker theory. The necessitation, I have suggested, is a world-to-proposition necessitation, not an entailment relation.

If every truth has a truthmaker, then this formula tells us what truth in general is. But I do not wish to call it a definition, because the right-hand side of the formula may involve the notion of truth. A fundamental concept such as truth is likely to be so entwined with other fundamental notions that no total explication of it in terms of other concepts is possible. But perhaps we can use the notion of a truth-condition (to be sharply distinguished from the notion of a truthmaker – a truth-condition is no more than a proposition) and say that what we have here is a necessary and sufficient truth-condition for truth.

2.9. TRUTHMAKERS FOR P MAY (PROPERLY) INCLUDE TRUTHMAKERS FOR P

Suppose p to be a truth and T to be a truthmaker for p. There may well exist, often there does exist, a T' that is contained by T, and a T''

that contains T, with T′ and T″ *also* truthmakers for *p*. We may say that truthmakers for a particular truth may be more or less *discerning*. The more embracing the truthmaker, the less discerning it is. For every truth, the least discerning of all truthmakers is the world itself, the totality of being. The world makes every truth true, or, failing that, every truth that has a truthmaker true. But this is an uninteresting truthmaker, mentioned here just for theoretical completeness.

It is necessary, though, to think carefully about these relations of inclusion among truthmakers for a particular truth. The obvious relation to identify it with is mereological inclusion, the simplest relation of whole and proper part. It will then be helpful, though perhaps not essential, to subscribe to the doctrine of Unrestricted Mereological Composition,[7] the thesis that any plurality of things, however heterogeneous, is a mereological whole. Then one can always have a single object as truthmaker. But however we settle that question, mereology may not be all that is needed. Some of us hold that there are in the world *facts* (states of affairs), entities having such forms as *a's being F* and *a's having R to b*. It is widely appreciated that these entities, if they exist, have a non-mereological form of composition (*a* and F might both exist, yet *a* not be F). Yet the state of affairs of *a's* being F seems to include, to have as constituents, the particular *a* and the property F. Furthermore, the constituents can be truthmakers on their own just as much as the states of affairs that contain them. It may be that there are other forms of composition in the world, though I myself am content with mereology and states of affairs.

This nesting of truthmakers for a particular truth may cast some light on the old idea that in a valid argument the conclusion is in some way contained in the totality of the premises. This is hard to make precise for the propositions that are linked as premises and conclusions in an argument. But if we consider *truthmakers* for these propositions perhaps something more interesting emerges. Suppose that a certain valid argument is *sound*, having all its premises true. Next we remind ourselves of the Entailment principle (see 2.5):

$$T \to p$$
$$\underline{p \text{ entails}^* q}$$
$$\therefore T \to q$$

---

[7] Elsewhere in my argument, however, I shall actually require the truth of Unrestricted Mereological Composition. It comes, I believe, with no ontological cost.

The plausible Containment thesis is then that for each T, p and q, T will have a part that is a truthmaker for q. We may count T as an (improper) part of itself, so already the conclusion $T' \to q$ is a case which fits the thesis. But very often, in particular where q does not entail p, we will have cases where q has a truthmaker, T', that is a *proper* part of T. Instead of conclusions contained in premises we have truthmakers for the conclusion contained in truthmakers for the premises. Or so the Containment principle asserts. I do not know if the principle holds for all cases, but it certainly holds in many cases. In particular it appears to hold for the (amended) Jackson principle (2.5) that links 'purely' contingent premises with contingent conclusions.

Consider, for instance, the traditional syllogism: <All men are mortal>, <Socrates is a man>, so <Socrates is mortal>. The truthmaker for the first premise is, I think, the mereological sum of all the earthly lives of all men, together with the totality state of affairs that this *is* the totality of such lives (for totality states of affairs see 6.2). Since all of them in fact end with a death, we have here already a (non-minimal) truthmaker for the death of Socrates. This truthmaker contains as a proper part the terminating of Socrates' life by death. The containment is in this case merely mereological, because the conjunction of each life is no more than a mereological sum of the lives, and Socrates' life is one of the conjuncts. But not all containment is mereological, at any rate if there are states of affairs (facts) in the furniture of the world. States of affairs have constituents (particulars, properties and relations) that seem to be parts of states of affairs, but not to be mereological parts.

Where propositions are false, we cannot have containment of truthmakers, but may still, of course, have valid arguments. Provided, however, that the false propositions involved are not impossibilities, we can 'go to possible worlds where the entailing proposition is true' and assert that, in general at least, the proposition's truthmakers in these worlds contain the truthmakers of anything it entails.

2.10. MINIMAL TRUTHMAKERS

We have introduced the least discerning truthmaker of them all, W, the world. It is also the most promiscuous truthmaker, for it makes every truth, or every truth that has a truthmaker, true. More interesting, and of quite special importance for metaphysics, is the notion of a minimal truthmaker. If T is a minimal truthmaker for p, then you cannot subtract anything from T and the remainder still be a truthmaker for *p*. Suppose, making some quite controversial assumptions for the sake of the example, that the truthmakers include properties, that these properties are universals, that universals are contingent existences, and that having rest-mass of one kilo is one such property. It is clear that this property is a truthmaker for the truth that this property exists. What is more, it is surely a minimal truthmaker.

It is interesting to look at certain metaphysical theories from the perspective of truthmaking theories, and to consider whether the account they offer of certain entities is a good candidate for a minimal truthmaker for the truth (as they take it to be) that these entities exist. David Lewis's ontology, as is well known, is exhausted by a *pluriverse* (the totality of being) consisting of all the possible worlds (Lewis, 1986). He defines a 'proposition' as the class of all the worlds for which the particular proposition is true. (Notice that his system does not allow for a null world, and hence he cannot form the class of the null worlds. As a result he cannot admit impossible propositions, a weakness, I would argue, because we can and do believe and assert impossibilities.) Suppose that one thinks of each of these worlds as the truthmaker for that proposition in that world. Let the proposition be that <cats catch mice>. It will be true in our actual world, and many other worlds. This gives us the class of worlds that Lewis identifies with the proposition that cats catch mice. But it is clear that this bunch of worlds is not a minimal truthmaker for the proposition, though it may be *a* truthmaker. (The mereological sum of episodes in our world involving the generality of cats catching mice when given the opportunity seems to be nearer to what is needed for a minimal truthmaker.)

Lewis, of course, is not trying to find a truthmaker for the truth of a proposition, such as the proposition <cats catch mice>. But I submit that in metaphysics we should primarily be concerned with truthmakers. And it is this, I think, that is responsible for the weird sound of Lewis's doctrine of propositions.

One might object to the idea that there are any truthmakers *except* minimal truthmakers. For, it may be argued, a non-minimal truthmaker involves redundancy, and the truth in question may *not* be true in virtue of the redundant material. This is a possible way to go, but I think that it is methodologically an unwise choice, for similar reasons to the logician's practice of taking 'some' not to exclude 'all'. In actual philosophical investigations it can be difficult to delineate the minimal truthmaker precisely while still being able to point to truthmakers that are non-minimal. But if someone wishes to say that what I call a non-minimal truthmaker for a certain proposition is really a portion of reality that has the real truthmaker as a proper part, then I have no metaphysical objection. It is to be noted in any case that there are certain propositions that may be true, but cannot have minimal truthmakers (see 2.12).

2.11. A TRUTH MAY HAVE MANY MINIMAL TRUTHMAKERS

One might think off-hand that a truth has only one minimal truthmaker. It is very important to notice that many, many truths have more than one minimal truthmaker. Consider the truth that a human being exists: <there exists an x such that x is a human being>. If we take existence omnitemporally (my own metaphysical preference, and one that will later be defended by truthmaker arguments – see ch. 11), then every human being that has ever existed, exists now or will exist in the future is a truthmaker for this truth. Furthermore, each of these human beings seems to be, or to be very close to being, a minimal truthmaker. (My caution here is because you could quite plausibly suggest that selected portions of human beings could be omitted from these truthmakers and yet you would still have enough to be a truthmaker for this truth!) If you want a cleaner example, consider the possibility that there is a plurality of simple properties. If this possibility actually obtains, then each simple property is a minimal truthmaker for the truth <there exist simple properties>.

We may note in passing that not only are there truths that have many different truthmakers, but that every truthmaker makes many truths true. Consider the case where p has a truthmaker. Truths of the form $<p \vee \_>$ will all be true in virtue of that truthmaker. A truthmaker is, indeed, an inexhaustible fountain of truths.

2.12. TRUTHS WITHOUT MINIMAL TRUTHMAKERS

Is it the case that for every truth there exists at least one minimal truthmaker? It sounds very plausible, but Greg Restall (1995) has given an ingenious counter-instance that makes it plausible that, provided the world contains at least a denumerable infinity of entities, then there are truths that have no minimal truthmaker. Suppose, for instance, that the world contains a denumerable infinity of electrons, and consider the truth <there exist an infinity of electrons>. The totality of electrons is a truthmaker for that truth. But take every third electron. That sub-totality makes the very same truth true, because the sub-totality is infinite. And so for the selection of the *n*th electron, where *n* is any finite natural number. Hence a minimal truthmaker is never reached. Any infinity in nature will make true certain truths that have no minimal truthmakers. Normally, however, a truth that has a truthmaker will have at least one minimal truthmaker.

Paul Horwich has pointed out, however, that there is a candidate for a minimal truthmaker even in the electron case (Horwich, 2003). Simply postulate a fact or state of affairs: *There exist an infinity of electrons.* Horwich himself has no sympathy with the notion of truthmaking, but his point is correct formally. If there is such a state of affairs, it will be a minimal truthmaker. Few upholders of the notion of truthmaker theory, though, would be likely to accept the truthmaker that Horwich offers. The state of affairs would be an extremely abstract one (in the traditional sense of the word 'abstract'). It would, for instance, sit very uneasily among the more concrete states of affairs involving particulars with their properties and the conjunctions of these states of affairs, which is a state of affairs metaphysics rather naturally deals in. It is difficult, for instance, to see any plausible causal role that could be given to a state of affairs of the sort suggested by Horwich. Nevertheless, Horwich's pointing out the formal possibility of postulating such a state of affairs serves as a useful reminder that, in passing from truths to truthmakers, no truthmaker is *automatically* picked out. No royal road to truthmakers!

I know of no other set of cases except certain truths involving infinity, such as the example given, where truths have truthmakers, but (plausibly) lack any minimal truthmaker. This result, however, does not completely stand by itself. When we come to discuss truthmakers for modal truths we shall see that it enables us to steer past a troubling, if minor, dilemma. See 7.5.

2.13. UNIQUE MINIMAL TRUTHMAKERS

It seems clear, then, that many truths have many minimal truthmakers. But there are cases where truths have one *and no more than one* minimal truthmaker. For instance, if there are states of affairs, such entities as *a*'s being F, with *a* a particular and F a genuine universal (or, for that matter, F a genuine trope), the truth <*a* is F> has that state of affairs as unique minimal truthmaker. The candidates for unique minimal truthmakers that a particular philosopher upholds take us into the heart of that thinker's metaphysical position. Where truthmakers are minimal but not unique, as in the case of the truth that a human being exists, it seems that the truth in question is always in some way 'abstract' (in the classical sense of this word, not Quine's 'not spatiotemporal').

In one way, therefore, it is very interesting what unique minimal truthmakers a philosopher postulates. In another way, it is rather boring, because the description of the truthmaker that we would naturally give will be reproduced in the statement of the truth. Here, according to that philosopher, the truth reflects the form of reality. And whatever the truthmakers are alleged to be, the following general statement can be made: for every truthmaker T, the truth <T exists> has T as its unique minimal truthmaker. The metaphysician's preferred list of Ts are the sorts of thing that, as Quine would put it, 'you are prepared to quantify over'. But bringing Quine into the matter demands further discussion.

2.14. THE POSTULATION OF TRUTHMAKERS CONTRASTED WITH 'QUANTIFYING OVER'

To postulate certain truthmakers for certain truths is to admit those truthmakers to one's ontology. The complete range of truthmakers admitted constitutes a metaphysics, which alerts us to the important point, stressed already but bearing much repetition, that the hunt for truthmakers is as controversial and difficult as the enterprise of metaphysics. I think that proceeding by looking for truthmakers is an illuminating and useful regimentation of the metaphysical enterprise, or at least the enterprise of a realist metaphysics. But it is no easy and automatic road to the truth in such matters.

But this raises the question of Quine, and the signalling of ontological commitment by what we are prepared to 'quantify over'. Why should we desert Quine's procedure for some other method? The great advantage, as I see it, of the search for truthmakers is that it focuses us not merely on the metaphysical implications of the subject terms of propositions but also on their *predicates*. Quine has told us that the predicate gives us 'ideology' rather than ontology (1966, p. 232).[8] This saying is rather dark, but it is clear that, to some degree, he has stacked the ontological deck against predicates as opposed to subject terms. But when we look to truthmakers

---

[8] Quine writes: 'In science all is tentative, all admits of revision . . . But ontology is, pending revision, more clearly in hand than what may be called *ideology* – the question of admissible predicates' (Quine, 1966, p. 232).

for truths, subject and predicate start as equals, and we can consider the ontological implications of both in an unbiased way.

The doing of ontological justice to the predicate leads us to consider whether we do not require at least selected properties and relations in our ontology. If properties and relations are admitted, we may think that some ontological connection between subjects and predicates is further required, and thus, perhaps, be led to postulate facts or states of affairs among our truthmakers. The propositional nature of truths will in any case push us in the same direction. The existence of negative truths and general truths raises the question whether negative and general facts are required as truthmakers. All these difficult metaphysical issues (which will receive discussion in chs. 5 and 6) tend to be swept under the carpet by correlating one's ontology with the subject term only of truths (what one takes to be truths).

Some may argue that what I see here as advantages of thinking in terms of truthmakers are actually disadvantages. The world is a world of things not of facts, it may be said, and so we do not want facts, and the nightmare of such entities as negative facts, in our ontology. This is an arguable position, of course, but, conceding it true for the sake of argument, it can still be accommodated by a doctrine of truthmakers. Let the world be a world of things. The fundamental truths (those that have unique minimal truthmakers) will then have the form 'X exists' and the Xs, whatever they may be, will be truthmakers for these truths.

2.15. DIFFERENT TRUTHS, SAME MINIMAL TRUTHMAKERS

Truths, we have seen, may have many minimal truthmakers. Is it the case that different truths can have the very same minimal truthmaker? (As we have noted, they all have the same maximal truthmaker, the world.) There are many examples. Trivial ones are easy to find. Just take some truth with a minimal truthmaker and add disjuncts where the additions are all false. The original minimal truthmaker will also serve for the new disjunctive truths. But there are more interesting cases. The propositions <*a*'s surface is scarlet> and <*a*'s surface is red> may both be true and, although the first truth necessitates the second truth, they are different truths. Yet the minimal truthmaker for both truths may well be the same: the possession by the surface of the exact shade of colour that it has.

Here is a more controversial sort of case. I will construct an artificial example because my point can then be made more clearly, but I think that there may be empirical examples: the philosophically famous case of the chicken sexers, and the ability of the old Mississippi river pilots to distinguish reefs from pseudo-reefs. (See Twain, 1962, pp. 62–3.)

Suppose, then, that a certain perceiver has the ability to spot regular pentagons, that is, decent approximations to the geometer's regular pentagons, and to distinguish them from other shapes, but has no ability to analyse the nature of the shape. This perceiver cannot count, and has quite undeveloped concepts of lines and angles. To this perceiver the shape is pretty well an unanalysed gestalt. 'Regular pentagon' would mean nothing to him, but he is still very proficient at picking the shape. Suppose he makes the true statement, or holds the belief, that a certain object has this shape that he can pick out so efficiently. He may even have his own predicate for this sort of shape. The truth that he has grasped is surely a different truth from ours when we say truly that the object is a regular pentagon. But the two truths may well have exactly the same minimal truthmaker, a unique minimal truthmaker.

It seems to be a necessary truth that the property picked out by this person is the regular pentagon shape. If we imagine that he later learns geometry, then he will rediscover this necessary truth <this shape is a regular pentagon> *a priori*.

Logical equivalences provide other, perhaps less interesting, cases of different truths with the same minimal truthmaker. Consider the truth (as we may here assume it to be) <all ravens are black>. Then consider its contrapositive: <all non-black things are non-ravens>. These truths are logically equivalent, and it is therefore very plausible to say that they have the very same minimal and all other truthmakers. But it is arguable, at least, that here we have different truths. No beginner in logic will be inclined to criticize this thesis!

So much for the 'general theory of truthmaking'. Some general points of methodology in the search for the true truthmakers are still to be introduced, and will come up in the course of the next chapter.

3

Epistemology and methodology

3.1. THE EPISTEMIC BASE

We have introduced the notion of a truthmaker, and discussed some of the formalities involved. But now we want to use it in metaphysics. This, however, brings up the question of the starting point. It is in virtue of truthmakers that truths are true, or so this essay argues. But in arriving at metaphysical results, it is truths, or, rather, it is what we take to be truths, that have to be our starting point. We take certain things to be true, and then ask what truthmakers these truths demand. It may be that at times we will think that we must have certain truthmakers, and as a result add to what we take to be our stock of truths. Or we might find ourselves unwilling to postulate certain truthmakers and therefore having to reject what we had previously taken to be truths. But, in general, in metaphysics the path is *from* supposed truth *to* truthmaker. So we need to consider at the beginning of a metaphysical investigation what we take to be true.

I suggest that in these circumstances it is reasonable to *start* by assuming truths in three areas: (1) the basic deliverances of common sense, what I call the Moorean truths, in recognition of the work of G. E. Moore; (2) secure results in logic and mathematics; (3) secure results in the natural sciences. We should now say something about these three bodies of truths. I believe that they give us, in Russell's phrase, the scope and limits of human knowledge.

3.2. MOOREAN TRUTHS

The term 'common sense' must be treated with caution. Many will hasten to point out that the common sense of mankind has been mistaken in the past on particular occasions and will undoubtedly be mistaken again from

Some of the material in this chapter is also covered in my Romanell Lecture (Armstrong, 1999b).

time to time. It was once part of common sense to think that the world is flat, that the sun literally rises and sets every day, and that simultaneity is an absolute conception, and so on. Here common sense was wrong.

But I am thinking of what perhaps may be called bedrock common sense. (And I think that is what Moore himself was thinking of.) Human beings have heads on their bodies, and hands and feet. They eat and drink, reproduce, and eventually die. They live in a world that contains, besides man-made things, other objects such as trees, rivers, mountains, winds, fires. These are *general* Moorean truths, and a good rough test for the members of this class is that it is almost embarrassing to mention them outside the context of philosophy. Each person, furthermore, has a stock of particular Moorean truths that do no more than overlap with the Moorean truths of others. It is a Moorean truth, part of my secure knowledge, that as I type these words it is late morning in Australia, in the suburb of Glebe in Sydney to be precise, and there are English words in front of me on a computer screen.

All Moorean knowledge is in many ways vague and imprecise. From the point of view of scientist or philosopher it is truth that involves extraordinarily little analysis or system. It is *surface* truth. But it is *epistemically* fundamental. It is the epistemically basic part of whatever knowledge we happen to have, and at one time, back in the state of nature, it was all that humanity had by way of a reliable epistemic base. It is what Descartes should have offered as an epistemic base instead of his *Cogito*. It is indeed Moorean knowledge for each of us that we exist (and, *pace* eliminativists, that we think). But our Moorean knowledge extends far beyond these two truths. Nor is the truth of the *Cogito* in any special epistemic position in the Moorean corpus. The true propositions <I am now thinking> and <I have a head on my shoulders> seem not to differ in certainty by any great degree. If anything, the latter proposition is more certain than the former: there are eliminativists about thoughts but not, I think, any school of thinkers who deny that we have heads on our shoulders.

We may note, as a piece of epistemology, that Moorean knowledge appears to be exclusively, or almost exclusively, based upon sense perception, the traditional 'five senses' plus the bodily perceptual systems. We do have some knowledge, via the faculty of introspection, of our own mental processes and states. But, following Locke and Kant, I would take this to be 'inner sense', with sense perception as 'outer sense', and so to be perception in a wide sense. In general, the answer to the question how Moorean knowledge is acquired seems to be the answer given by

27

empiricism: viz. from experience. There may be some innate contribution to Moorean knowledge, perhaps programmed by our evolutionary past, but that contribution cannot be very extensive.

Moorean knowledge is, of course, not logically indubitable knowledge, but it is in a more ordinary sense indubitable. No sane enquirer in fact doubts it. To the sceptic who challenges its claim to be knowledge we can say, as Moore said, that there is nothing outside it, in particular there is no *reasoning* starting either from alleged fact or theory that can rationally challenge it. For any premises the sceptic uses for the sceptical argument, however ingenious the argument may be, will be less certain than the Moorean corpus. (See Lycan, 2001, for a telling exposition of Moore's argument.) Indeed, the more ingenious the argument is, the more confident can we be that there is a flaw in it *somewhere*. (Though some qualification of this will be necessary shortly.)

Zeno's wonderful paradoxes are a good paradigm here. It is a Moorean truth that objects move. We should not allow Zeno, or anybody else, to persuade us of the contrary. What the paradoxes do is to show us that the question of the *nature* of motion can be an exceedingly thorny question, one that is not easily answered. I may add that it seems to me that the question of the nature of motion is unlikely to be settled by any mere process of thought, such as the thought of philosophers, but will depend on very deep physical investigations into the nature of things. Motion exists. That is Moorean truth. But this is compatible, perfectly compatible, with the nature of motion being a philosophical and/or scientific mystery. Moore himself was well aware of this sort of point. He would have said that although it was certain that things move, nevertheless the *analysis* of the nature of motion may still be an uncertain matter. From the standpoint of truthmaker theory we can say: the exact nature of the truthmaker for <motion exists> may still be to seek, and this exact nature may be quite a surprise.

The existence of motion appears to me to be unassailable. I do not, however, wish to deny that from time to time apparent Moorean truths may turn out to be falsities. Examples will now be discussed. But to show that certain apparent Moorean truths are not really true rational arguments are required, and the premises of these arguments must always rely on *other* parts of the Moorean corpus.

Consider, for instance, the proposition that the sun rises and sets every day. Was not this once part of common sense? But the words 'rising' and 'setting' carry the implication that the sun moves around the earth. And that, we now know, is false. The sun may appear to rise and to set, but it does not really do these things. So is this not a case of a proposition that is Moorean but false?

It seems, though, that we can, and we do, *purge* these ways of speaking. In thought we *cancel* this bad theory, and what is then left is Moorean *knowledge*: knowledge that these phenomena of 'the sun rising' and 'the sun setting' are physical matters of regular occurrence. The original 'common-sense' proposition splits into two: first, the existence of an undeniable regular happening involving earth and sun, a happening perceived by all who have eyes to see; second, a false description of what this happening is.

A trickier case, though, is presented by Sir Arthur Eddington's paradox of the 'two tables'. The surface of an ordinary table in reasonable condition is, to common sense, a plenum. There are no holes in it. Yet the 'scientific table', we are reliably assured by physics, is *mostly empty space*. (The most spectacular piece of evidence for this, I think, is that a beam of electrons can be shot through the table and in the vast majority of cases the beam will not be deflected in any way.) This is a case where an apparent Moorean truth has actually to be discarded in the light of scientific discovery. We do have the Moorean knowledge that the table *appears* to us to be a plenum. Furthermore, we have a good deal of Moorean knowledge concerning the apparent plenum. In particular, we know that it is both cognitively impenetrable to perception and physically impenetrable to ordinary objects such as cups, plates and books.

But much more important, to establish that the table is not a plenum physicists have to rely on the general correctness of the Moorean corpus at every point. Consider what leads physicists to say that there are electrons, and to say that beams of these particles can be fired through the table with little risk of hitting anything. This evidence must ultimately come from experiments and observations made in laboratories and elsewhere, and afterwards communicated to the community of physical scientists and others. If something of that sort had not been done, we would have had no reason to think that tables were so strangely empty. But then consider the innumerably many Moorean propositions that must hold up for the scientists – right down to where their laboratories are! – if they are to end up with good reasons for contradicting this one small part of the Moorean corpus.

I add a final note before finishing this section. One thing that should be obvious about Moorean knowledge, but perhaps should be said explicitly, is that the *theory* of Moorean knowledge, in particular the theorizing of this section, is not itself a case of such knowledge. What I have just been engaged in is philosophy, and philosophy is so far from containing any Moorean knowledge that it probably does not contain any *knowledge* at all, unless it be historical knowledge.

3.3. THE RATIONAL SCIENCES

Moorean truths, I suggest, are the ultimate foundations of all our knowledge. But moving beyond the Moorean truths, we come to the sciences, which may be divided in turn into the *rational* and the *empirical* sciences. It is characteristic of the rational sciences, logic and mathematics, that they enjoy a certainty that, while not absolute, is greater than that enjoyed by the natural sciences, that is, the empirical sciences.

In making this division, I am assuming that there is a fundamental difference between the two sorts of discipline, and this is controversial, certainly in philosophy and perhaps elsewhere. Philosophers such as Quine see the difference as no more than a difference of degree. It is a matter, perhaps, of the greater metaphorical 'distance' that one set of propositions, the logical and mathematical truths, have from experience. It reflects no more than a greater or less unwillingness to revise accepted propositions in the light of potentially recalcitrant experience. I should therefore emphasize that my division of the sciences into the rational and the empirical disciplines, like the rest of my argument in this chapter, is not to be accounted part of the Moorean consensus that constitutes our epistemic base. The division, in particular, is a piece of philosophy, and the propositions of philosophy are certainly not part of our epistemic base!

However, my reasons for making a sharp distinction between the rational and the empirical sciences are reasons that perhaps the majority of philosophers, or indeed other rational thinkers, will be sympathetic with. The truths of logic and mathematics are discovered, at least in very high degree, by *a priori* methods. They are discovered by thought and by calculation (nowadays sometimes by calculator or computer), and, characteristically, they are *proved*.[1] Proof is not a logically indubitable process, for there is no logically indubitable method of attaining truth. But that does

---

[1] The value of proof had to be discovered, of course. It was discovered by the Greeks, and proof theory has been refined by contemporary logic and mathematics. It is interesting to recall that the Indian mathematical genius Ramanujan had to be taught proof theory by G. H. Hardy. See Kanigel, 1992, pp. 220–5.

not mean that purported proofs in this area do not have an extremely high degree of reliability. After proofs have been thoroughly checked by the relevant experts in the field, you can, as the horse-racing commentators say, put down your glasses.

In regimented proof, of course, proof requires axioms. What their status is I will largely pass over here, although it is important to say that they are not indubitable. Because of the simplicity and precision demanded of axioms it seems unlikely that any of them are Moorean truths, which are characteristically imprecise.

The central role for proof, and ultimately proof from axioms, is in sharp contrast to the application of logic and mathematics in the empirical sciences. This application, of course, is an ever-increasing part of those sciences. The 'unreasonable effectiveness of mathematics' in the empirical sciences (Eugene Wigner's phrase) keeps being demonstrated,[2] and it does seem an enormous surprise, a surprise that could not have been foreseen *a priori*, that mathematics is so very, very effective in empirical investigation. I have no explanation for this, except that the world has turned out to be like this. It is pretty mysterious. But whatever deductions are made from mathematically formulated hypotheses about the world of nature, in the end the resulting conclusions still have to be tested *against* observation. This sets a great gulf between the rational and the empirical sciences.

This distinction between the *a priori* sciences of mathematics and logic, on the one hand, and the *a posteriori* nature of the empirical sciences, on the other, raises philosophical problems, of course. I think that Kant's question, or rather a somewhat wider variant of Kant's question, viz. the question 'How is *a priori* knowledge possible?' is a thoroughly justified question, and sets a very difficult problem for empiricists such as myself. It does seem quite clear that logic and mathematics are bodies of knowledge on which we can rely, fairly clear that they are *a priori* disciplines, and at least plausible that they are bodies of necessary truths. And in any case the (secure) results of these disciplines are part of the proper epistemic base in philosophy, even if these results are not so epistemically prior as our Moorean knowledge.

An attempt to answer the Kantian question will be made in section 8.2.

---

[2] See Wigner, 1960, and for some qualifications, see Hamming, 1980. I thank James Franklin for the references.

3.4. THE EMPIRICAL SCIENCES

Turning to the empirical sciences, we should draw a distinction between the *frontiers* of science and the settled body of knowledge that is presupposed by those working at the frontiers. This distinction may have its place in the rational sciences of mathematics and logic, but that place is much smaller than in the natural sciences. There are conjectures in logic and mathematics, of course, but once a proof or disproof of a conjecture has been proposed it is not long before frontiers become settled territory. Even in the horribly difficult case of Fermat's last theorem, it was only a matter of two or three years before the originally suggested, but faulty, proof was improved and the resulting proof accepted by the experts. In the empirical sciences matters regularly remain controversial, in greater or lesser degree, for a very much longer time. Even apparently very well established results, such as Newton's law of gravitation once seemed to be, can turn out to be no more than good approximations to the truth under a wide range of observable conditions. And the achieving of these new results can send reverberations back concerning the truth-value of what was before accounted secure knowledge. Nevertheless, there are established results. It is *known* that water is composed of water molecules, and that these molecules are made up of two atoms of hydrogen and one of oxygen. It is *known* that mankind has evolved over a great period of time, from simpler organisms, and (perhaps to trail my coat a little) *known* that the causal mechanism of natural selection has played a very considerable part, at least, in that evolution. And for many scientific propositions where knowledge is lacking, there can be rational belief, cases where a high degree of rational assurance can be assigned to that belief.

3.5. DEFLATIONARY TRUTHMAKERS

Here, then, in Moorean knowledge, in what has been proved in mathematics and logic, and in what is known or rationally believed in the natural sciences, we find our proper epistemic base. I do not believe that we have any other knowledge, at least knowledge of a reliable sort. Here there is what we might call the (current) rational consensus. For these truths or apparent truths, we must propose truthmakers in our metaphysics, truthmakers that do not threaten this epistemic base. It is a further question, though, an important question in epistemology and a difficult one, what are the epistemic principles that *justify* our claiming this as the proper

32

epistemic base. I hope that what has been said already has begun the process of justification, but I will not pursue the matter further here. It is quite a good methodological principle not to get caught up in the questions raised by philosophical scepticism when engaged in metaphysics!

But I do wish to argue that in metaphysics we have a certain latitude in what we assign as truthmakers for particular truths. I am emphatically not saying that we create the truthmakers. They are just there or not there, whatever our opinion about them is. But I do assert that when assigning purported truthmakers there can very reasonably be disagreement among metaphysicians (who are going to disagree anyway) about what the truthmakers for certain truths are. Are mere uniformities in the world sufficient to provide truthmakers for true nomic (law) statements? Do mere classes of instances provide truthmakers for truths that things have properties? As we know, these matters are controversial (among philosophers) in the highest degree.

The particular examples just given are examples of what may be called *deflationary* truthmakers for the truths, which they are supposed to make true. They are deflationary because it is quite natural, when first faced with such theories, to think that the real truthmakers must be more than just that. Surely there is more than just regular succession to nomic connection? Surely there is more to a particular's having a property, say a certain mass, than its just being a member of a certain class of particulars?

As it happens, I think that in these cases the suggested deflationary truthmakers *are* insufficient. But I think that for certain truths deflationary truthmakers may provide the right answer. Indeed, I doubt that any plausible metaphysic can be put forward which does not appeal to deflationary truthmakers *at certain points*. What one should hope to do, though, where deflationary truthmakers are appealed to, is to find some plausible reason why we are tempted in these cases to look for something more robust.

The providing of deflationary truthmakers is to be distinguished from an *eliminativist* strategy, where certain apparent truths, say the proposition that mental entities exist, are said to be false. Eliminativists usually provide what one might think of as 'counterpart' truths that correspond to a degree to the propositions that they hold to be false. Thus, eliminativists about the mind normally concede that there are certain entities, viz. states and processes in the brain, that have many of the characteristics that mental things were supposed to have. The disagreement between deflationary and eliminativist accounts of the same matter can then become purely verbal. In these circumstances, while recognizing that the deflationary/eliminativist distinction is a matter of degree, I favour wherever possible going for deflationary rather than eliminativist accounts. Do not say that the sun never rises, say rather that it does rise, but that the truthmaker for this truth is not quite what the uninitiated might think. Pour the new wine into old bottles. It is, for instance, very inconvenient and on the whole misleading to have to deny that anybody does any action freely, even for those who think it likely that every event has a determining cause. A reduced or unambitious truthmaker, a somewhat deflationary truthmaker, such as one finds in the compatibilist defence of free will, therefore recommends itself. (The unambitious truthmakers are the existence of mental events of choosing between alternatives, something that is surely part of the Moorean corpus, whatever analysis we give of choosing. Furthermore, it is fairly obvious that in some of these choosings we are *relatively* uncoerced by other persons or by the environment. So there is free will, at least in this deflationary or minimalist sense.) In the particular case of eliminativism about the mental, however, I believe that this position goes clear against our Moorean assurance that there are such things as pains, perceptions and beliefs.

3.6. GOING BEYOND THE RATIONAL CONSENSUS

We come now to a very important point, one that I have learnt from Peter van Inwagen.[3] We all hold beliefs, he points out, on matters that go beyond what we might call the rational consensus that is to be found in Moorean knowledge, in matters proved in logic and mathematics, and in the securer parts of the natural sciences. His particular interest in making this point springs from his religious beliefs, but he points out quite rightly that secularists such as myself hold beliefs about political, social and moral matters that go well beyond what I am here claiming to be the proper epistemic base for claims of knowledge. And these are beliefs that we are not going to give up, even although we know perfectly well that they are disputed, disputed among those who are in the best position to know and judge the state of the argument. 'Nature', says Hume, 'by an absolute and uncontrollable necessity has determined us to judge as well as to breathe and feel' (*Treatise*, bk. I, pt. iv, sec. 1). And among those things that we judge about, judging in a pretty peremptory and unembarrassed manner,

---

[3] Van Inwagen, 1996.

are matters that we recognize with part of our mind to be thoroughly controversial, and not part of the rational consensus.

Van Inwagen might have gone on to point out that one place where this is much in evidence is within the discipline of philosophy itself. We, the practitioners of philosophy, think of it as a rational activity, but it does not issue in a consensus. Yet that does not stop us from upholding our own opinions in the most vigorous and obstinate way.

Such behaviour, however, even though we may rightly deplore certain particular manifestations of it, is not irrational. We have here, indeed, a case of what Hegel called 'the cunning of reason', by which he meant reason setting the passions to work for its own ends (Hegel, 1956 [1840], p. 33). Belief not only can and does, but in very many cases *should*, run ahead of knowledge, ahead of the rational consensus. In particular, competing beliefs are regularly necessary if knowledge on controversial matters is to be attained. Without believers in a theory, the theory is very unlikely to have its best face put forward, to have 'protective belts' of auxiliary hypotheses articulated and defended, and so to have its full power revealed to all. (Compare government by discussion, and also the free market.)

All the same, it seems desirable in philosophy and elsewhere that we should retain a feeling for where there really is knowledge and where there is only more or less rational belief. All that can be demanded is that we try to be as aware as we can be of when we are assuming something that is properly, rationally, to be regarded as controversial. I suggest, further, that we should be very chary of making *claims* to knowledge outside the rational consensus. I deliberately speak of claims. Many claim to know that God, the Christian God let us say, exists. Many would also claim to know that such a God does not exist. (Though I myself, fairly strongly inclining to the atheist position as I do, nevertheless do not claim *knowledge* that there is no God. To that extent I am an agnostic.) It is possible, I would concede (epistemically possible), that some persons in one or the other of these two camps do know what they claim to know. In just the same way, it is epistemically possible among the competing doctrines of the philosophers that some of us not merely hold a true belief on certain philosophical matters but actually *know* that truth. Let this be conceded. Nevertheless, I do not think that it is rational for any of the contending persons, in religion or in philosophy, publicly to *claim* knowledge. For though they *may* know (I am prepared to concede), it is hard to see how they can know that they know. A quiet hope that they really do have knowledge will be best.

35

3.7. TRUTHMAKERS THAT ARE TOO NARROW OR TOO WIDE

Metaphysics is not easy, and the hunt for truthmakers is not easy. One would like to get to minimal truthmakers where one can, but one may fall short in one's endeavour. The suggested truthmaker may be too *narrow*, that is to say, it may be no more than some necessary proper part of a minimal truthmaker for the truth in question. *Faute de mieux*, that will be progress. An example. In the past I have argued that the truthmaker for a dispositional truth such as 'This glass is brittle' is some categorical, non-dispositional state of the glass in question. At that time I had not made explicit to myself the idea that a truthmaker ought to necessitate its truths. But it still seems to me that such a categorical state is a *proper part* of the true truthmaker. Given that nomic truths are contingent, as I take them to be, the categorical state of the glass could be the same, yet the glass would be brittle in a world with different laws of nature. So, as I see it now, the truthmakers for the relevant nomic truths – those nomic truths that ensure that the glass behaves as brittle things behave – need to be added to the categorical state to yield a satisfactory truthmaker. (Of course, this example may be disputed, and is disputed by many contemporaries.)

In the same fashion, suggested minimal truthmakers may be truthmakers for the truth in question, but not in fact minimal ones. They will be too *wide*. Thus, it is often suggested by those who think about truthmakers that the whole world is required as a *minimal* truthmaker for such truths as <unicorns do not exist>. In fact, as I shall argue at 6.2.1, this appears not to be the case. A pretty extensive truthmaker is required for such truths, as is quite generally the case with negative truths, but not the whole world. It may still be valuable, nevertheless, to start with the larger truthmaker and work inwards towards minimal truthmakers.

An even more interesting sort of case is that where the minimal truthmaker has been correctly identified, but different parties to the metaphysical dispute give different accounts of the nature of this truthmaker. Each human being is perhaps a minimal or near to a minimal truthmaker for the truth <some human being exists>. But what is a human being? Different metaphysics will give different answers. A materialist philosopher who also rejects properties and relations *in re*, whether they are universals or particulars, might see a human being as no more than a physical thing, divisible into other physical things. But if *properties* and *relations* are thought to be required, then the truthmaker will have to be a much more structured affair, with the exact nature of this structure to be argued over further. A lot will depend upon what plausible truthmakers can be found for truths that 'attribute properties to particulars'. The opponent of properties and relations *in re* will have to provide truthmakers that do not involve these entities. In the next chapter we will plunge into some of these sorts of dispute.

3.8. METAPHYSICS AND EPISTEMOLOGY

Metaphysical and epistemological theory must inevitably interact. If one is considering the matter in the context of the theory of truthmakers, then the matter looks like this. The truth/truthmaking relation is, in a broad sense, a semantic relation. To find truthmakers for certain truths, or sorts of truths, one wants to postulate entities that stand in various more or less complex relations of correspondence to these truths. But one wants these entities to be such that we can know, or at least have rational belief, that such entities exist. The entities must be such that they are epistemically accessible.

Looking at the epistemological problem from a naturalist perspective, which takes knowledge and rational belief to be natural phenomena, then the obvious thing to do is to look for some causal or at least some nomic link between the postulated truthmakers and the truths that we can fairly claim to know or to rationally believe. If, for instance, portions of the world, some of the truthmakers, are able to affect our minds in such a way as to create in us a more or less reliable belief that these truthmakers exist, then, perhaps, we will be able to marry metaphysics and epistemology in a plausible manner.

This is the pragmatic, by which I mean non-apodeictic, justification for adopting what Graham Oddie (1982) has christened the Eleatic Principle (after the Eleatic Stranger in Plato's *Sophist*). The principle is perhaps best stated by saying that everything that we postulate to exist should make *some sort* of contribution to the causal/nomic order of the world. The *some sort* is to be emphasized; there may be all sorts of ways that an entity makes this contribution. Particulars, properties, states of affairs, causes and laws themselves all make their contribution, but make them in different ways. We can use David Lewis's useful phrase that he introduced in his philosophy of mind: these entities have different *causal roles*. Yet without some causal and/or nomic contribution it is at least not easy to see how we can come to know of, or at least have rational belief in, their existence.

I can (alas!) see no contradiction in the notion of epiphenomenal entities, whether they be particulars or properties. The Eleatic Principle seems not to be a necessary truth. But I cannot see what rational grounds there are for postulating anything epiphenomenal.

The moral for truthmaker theory is obvious. We should turn our back on such truthmakers as other possible worlds, and any other transcendent entities that are not credited with causal powers *in this world*.

4

Properties, relations and states of affairs

We have introduced the topic of truthmakers, given an informal presentation of some of its formalities, and sketched some of the methodological and epistemological points that, in my view, should be borne in mind in the search for suitable truthmakers. So far, except for the recommendation that whatever truthmakers are postulated should make some sort of causal/nomic contribution to the working of the actual world, the points made have been relatively neutral with respect to the truthmakers that it is desirable to postulate. This is now to change. It is my belief that if one follows out the implications of a truthmaker approach as set out in the previous chapters one will be led fairly naturally (especially if one leans towards empiricism and naturalism) to a series of particular solutions to the question what truthmakers we should postulate (and in particular what minimal truthmakers we should postulate) in arriving at an ontology. A good place to begin is with the theory of properties.

4.2. PROPERTIES

In our discourse, we predicate all sorts of things of all sorts of subjects, and some of these predications are perhaps not of great ontological importance. ('Identical with itself' may be a good example of an unimportant predication. The truthmaker for <*a* is identical with itself> seems to be just *a*.) But let us consider a case where a certain particular has a certain mass, four kilograms exact, say, truly predicated of it. What is the truthmaker for this truth?

An obvious *first* answer is 'Just the particular itself.' Such a particular will be insufficient as truthmaker if attributing a certain mass to a body makes covert reference to some further particular. In that case, the property will be, to a degree at least, a relational property, and such properties essentially involve further particulars. It is at least quite plausible, however, to think that mass properties do not in fact demand further particulars in this way. So we will assume for the sake of argument that mass is a non-relational property (intrinsic property, as some say) of the particular. Under the guidance of physics we might at some future time wish to challenge this assumption. But suppose here that the assumption is true. Then the particular by itself is a sufficient truthmaker for the truth that it has this mass. It may not be a *minimal* truthmaker – that point remains to discuss – but it is a truthmaker.

At this point, however, we should remind ourselves that there are certain nominalist metaphysics – the extremer ones – that actually seem to *demand* going outside the particular even in the case of a non-relational property. (I mean by a nominalist metaphysic one that holds that *everything* that exists is a particular and nothing more than a particular.) For some of these extreme nominalists, the particular has that mass because it is a member of a certain class of particulars, the class we would naturally describe as consisting of all and only all those particulars that have that mass. (I call this position Class Nominalism.) For others, the particular has that mass because the predicate 'mass of four kilos exact' applies to, or is true of, that particular (Predicate Nominalism).

It is natural to suppose, once we start thinking in terms of truthmakers, that for a Class Nominalist *the class of all the four-kilo objects* is the truthmaker for the truth that the particular has just that mass. Yet this suggested truthmaker looks far too big! Would not the object still be four kilos in mass even if the other members of the class had never existed?[1] In the case of Predicate Nominalism, it is suggested that the predicate, a meaningful linguistic expression, must be brought into the truthmaker along with the object, together presumably with the 'applying to' or 'true of' relation that holds between that predicate and that object. But, once again, will not the object suffice *by itself*? It would have the same mass, whether or not the predicate existed.

It is useful to pose the *Euthyphro* dilemma here. It is in many ways the most useful dilemma in metaphysics, and the argument of this essay will rely on it at a number of points.[2] Consider, first, the class of the objects that are just four kilos in mass. Do the members of the class have the

---

[1] This will perhaps need to be qualified. See 4.5.

[2] At 2.6, we already met a case where the Euthyphro dilemma can usefully be put. Should we say that sentences have the same meaning in virtue of their membership of classes of synonymous sentences? Or should we say that sentences fall into such classes in virtue of

property of being just four kilos in mass in virtue of membership of this class? Or is it rather that they are members of this class in virtue of each having this mass-property? The latter view seems much more attractive. The class could have had different members, but the mass-property would be the same, it would seem. Again, does the object have this property in virtue of the application a predicate, or is the predicate applied in virtue of the property? The former view seems near to madness. The object would have had the property even if the predicate had never existed.

The situation with Resemblance Nominalism, the theory that a thing's properties are somehow constituted by the resemblance, greater or less resemblance, that it bears to other particulars, might seem to be unsatisfactory for the same reason. But I do not think that this is so. For it seems fairly clear that the resemblance of things is determined by the natures of the resembling things, although different accounts may be given of *nature* here. Resemblance seems to be an internal relation, necessitated by the terms of the related things. We are then back at the thing itself as truthmaker. That, I think, is a score for the Resemblance Nominalist when compared to Class and Predicate Nominalisms.[3]

But even 'the thing itself' seems not to be a *minimal* truthmaker for the thing's having the particular mass that it has. After all, we want to say that the thing has a great many other properties. In particular, it has a great many other non-relational properties, properties where no *further* entities seem required as truthmakers to make it true that it has the property. It has, for instance, a certain shape, a certain size, a certain temperature, a certain chemical constitution. Along with mass, these properties seem, at least, to be non-relational. Is it the *entire thing* that is needed each time as truthmaker to make each of these different predications true?

It is at this point that it becomes entirely natural and reasonable to postulate that the object has properties that are objectively there, and that one or more of these properties is the truthmaker for saying truly that it has a mass of four kilograms, another for saying that it has a certain shape, still another that it has a certain temperature, and another property or properties for saying that it has a certain chemical constitution. There is, of course, the question just how we decide what are the true or real properties. There is also, as we have noted, the question just how we decide

each sentence having the same meaning? Marian David has pointed out how much more plausible is the second rather than the first view.

[3] A striking attempt to rehabilitate Resemblance Nominalism against a number of traditional criticisms has been made by Gonzalo Rodriguez-Pereyra. See his 2002.

41

that we are really dealing with *non-relational* properties. My own answer is that we settle both these matters, so far as we can do it, in the light of total science. Philosophy has to take a back seat.

4.2.1. Different conceptions of properties

Truthmaking considerations, I have just been arguing, seem to favour a *realism* about properties, at least for many cases where a predicate attaches truly to an object. It is important to see, though, that such a realism is compatible with different accounts of these properties that are 'really there'. First, there is the now familiar distinction between properties taken to be universals and properties taken to be particulars. Ordinary discourse is regularly found attributing the 'same' property to different objects. Different particulars are *both* said to have the same mass. A believer in universals holds that this is identity in a strict sense. In technical phrase: two objects may instantiate the very same universal. Those nominalists who nevertheless accept realism about properties ('moderate nominalism' seems a good label) argue that the word 'same' here must be understood in some looser sense, one compatible with the denial of universals. Each four-kilo object has its *own* mass. Donald Williams's word 'trope' has become more or less the standard term for these particularized properties. It is not an entirely suitable term, but like democratic government or long life it is on the whole better than the other options on offer. Tropes may resemble each other to a greater or lesser degree, including *exact* resemblance. Exact resemblance is symmetrical, transitive and reflexive, thus permitting equivalence classes of exactly resembling tropes. Membership of such a class of tropes can then be proposed as an alternative to the strict identity upheld by believers in universals. (It is also possible, but not very common, to accept both sorts of property – both universal and trope – into one's ontology. There seems to be a failure of economy in this view.)

A word about universals before we move on. A theory that has particulars instantiating *transcendent* universals seems to put properties 'outside' their particulars. It offends against the original insight that the *thing itself* should serve as truthmaker, even if not as minimal truthmaker, for truths that particulars have certain (non-relational) properties. A theory of *immanent* universals is required if the truthmaker for a non-relational property of a particular is to be found 'within the particular'.

There is another distinction, which yields two theories of properties, a distinction that is independent of, and cuts across, the question of universals versus tropes. Are we to think of properties as powers, causal powers, to produce further effects under suitable circumstances? Or should we think of them as having an existence that is independent of the powers that they bestow upon particulars that have these properties? Terminology is less fixed here, but we can call this the *dispositionalist* versus the *categoricalist* conception of properties. Once again, this distinction allows for mixed views: one can, for instance, take a 'two-sided' view of all properties, giving them both a power side and a categorical side. Dispositionalist views, when developed, tend (but only tend) to produce postulations of necessities *in re* in the situations where the powers are exercised.

My object in introducing these difficult disputes – universals versus tropes, dispositionalism versus categoricalism – is not to try to decide them here, but to indicate the *limits* to truthmaker thinking. (There will, however, be need to advert to these different theories from time to time.) It is clear, I think, that these disputes are disputes about ontology. Different truthmakers are postulated for truths about properties. I have claimed that thinking in terms of truthmakers favours (without clearly necessitating) some realist theory of properties. But when we come to the fine structure of the ontology of properties – illustrated by the theories adumbrated in the two previous paragraphs – then truthmaking theory does not seem of very great help in reaching a decision between the competing theories. Continually to raise the truthmaker question about properties makes for ontological honesty. I have just argued that realist theories of properties seem required for a good answer. But arguing for a particular position inside the 'space' of the various realist theories of properties demands more fine-spun argumentation. I have embarked on that elsewhere, and will largely, though not entirely, pass it by here.

4.2.2. A difficulty for trope theories?

The battle between upholders of tropes and upholders of universals has gone on and on in contemporary metaphysics. It is generally agreed that *both* theories, suitably articulated, can do a great deal of justice to what needs to be explained concerning predicates and properties. Herbert Hochberg, however, has produced an argument that seems to me to be a problem for trope theories. (See his 2001, pp. 69–70.) Because it is a truthmaker argument, it is of interest to consider it here.

Hochberg starts from what he takes to be 'a fundamental principle of ontological analysis' that 'logically independent basic statements require different truth makers' (n.92). I am not sure if this principle will hold up. I prefer to argue simply from a case. Hochberg considers the case of two *simple* but exactly resembling tropes. We will call them '*a*' and '*b*'. Given the existence of *a* and *b*, then it is a truth, a necessary truth, that <*a* is diverse from *b*>. I would say that the truthmakers are just the mereological sum of the terms: *a* + *b*. Hochberg would disagree, but this disagreement does not seem important for the purposes of this argument. Given the existence of *a* and *b*, then it is, by hypothesis, a truth that <*a* is exactly similar to *b*>. Again I would say that the truthmakers are *a* + *b*: the very same truthmakers for the two different truths. Given that *a* and *b* are simples, this seems counter-intuitive.

I do not want to say that such a situation can be condemned *a priori*. We have seen in chapter 2 that the relations between truths and truthmakers permit all sorts of complexity. But neither truth can be derived from the other. (In particular, the diversity cannot be derived from the exact similarity, because any trope is exactly similar to itself.) Each of the simple entities is the truthmaker for (i) its difference from the other simple entity and (ii) its exact similarity. It seems highly suspicious that these two *simple* entities are grounds for these two truths. Does it not suggest that the allegedly simple trope has an inner complexity?

This leads me to suggest that tropes should really be assayed (to use the old Iowan term in honour of Hochberg) as *states of affairs* or *facts*. They are really a matter of particulars *having* properties. They contain within themselves both particulars and properties. States of affairs themselves should, I hold, be assayed as *particulars* (the 'victory of particularity', see my 1997, 8.4) and if this further point is correct then it does justice to the key idea associated with tropes: that they are particulars not universals.

4.2.3. *How do properties stand to the particulars that have them?*

Another important metaphysical issue is raised by taking a realist view of properties. A particular has such and such properties. How are we to conceive the particular itself? Is it something that has the properties? Or may it be reduced to a bundle of its properties? We must choose, in other words, between a substance/attribute account of the particular/property distinction, or else view a particular as a bundle of properties. Here is another very important ontological point of choice, one that is still largely independent of the choice between universals and tropes, and that between

TABLE 4.1

Universals or Tropes	Disp. or Categ.	Subs./Att. or Bundle
1. Universals	Dispositionalism	Substance/Attribute
2. Universals	Dispositionalism	Bundle
3. Universals	Categoricalism	Substance/Attribute
4. Universals	Categoricalism	Bundle
5. Tropes	Dispositionalism	Substance/Attribute
6. Tropes	Dispositionalism	Bundle
7. Tropes	Categoricalism	Substance/Attribute
8. Tropes	Categoricalism	Bundle

dispositional and categorical properties. It may be worth exhibiting the eight possibilities, reading across table 4.1.

All of these eight packages have their recommendations (and shortcomings), and, for the majority of these eight packages (by five to three at minimum), good philosophers can be found who have embraced one of them. For instance, (1) – power universals instantiated by particulars – is the theory embraced by Sydney Shoemaker (1984) and, more recently, Brian Ellis (2001); (2) – bundles of power universals – *may* be the view of Richard Holton (1999); (3) – categorical universals instantiated by particulars – may have been Aristotle's view and, along with many other philosophers, is mine (Armstrong, 1978, 1989b); (4) – bundles of categorical universals – Russell in his later philosophizing seems to have held a version of this view (1959, ch. 14; see also Hochberg, 1984); (5) – power tropes instantiated by particulars – is the view of C. B. Martin (1993) and John Heil (2003, chs. 8 and 10.6); (6) – bundles of power tropes – and (7) – categorical tropes instantiated by particulars – may be empty of actual upholders; (8) – bundles of categorical tropes – is the account favoured by Donald Williams, Keith Campbell, Peter Simons and many others (Williams, 1966, ch. 7; Campbell, 1990; Simons, 1994). All eight seem to be genuinely different theories, postulating different truthmakers. Choosing between them is delicate work. (And, of course, some solutions may well cross the boundaries set up in the table.) Truthmaker theory distinguishes the theories, but seems to help only a little in choosing the winner.

4.3. PREDICATION NECESSARY OR CONTINGENT?

But that is not the end to the different ways of dividing up the field of theories with respect to properties. Consider the way a property of a particular stands to the particular. In the classical analytic tradition this is thought of, with the possible exception of essential properties, as a contingent matter. But in recent years some have questioned this. Consider trope theories, in particular. Among those who accept trope theories of properties but make them attributes of substances are C. B. Martin and John Heil. They hold what Martin has called *non-transferable* theories of these properties-as-particulars. It is clear that if one wishes to refer to a particular trope then by far the most convenient way to do so will be to mention the particular it is an attribute of. It is, for instance, the mass of *this stone*. But the idea of non-transferability goes beyond this. The idea is that the mass is held to be the mass of this stone *by necessity*. It is an identity condition for the property. Every property then becomes an essential property.

This does not remove contingency from the world. The particular might not have existed, and then the trope would not have existed. It would seem also that the particular might have existed while the trope did not exist, though this may demand more thought. (Would the particular still be the same particular?) But given the particular and the trope, then the mass must be the mass of this stone.

Suppose that we turn instead to the position that ordinary particulars are not to be given a subject-attribute analysis, but are rather mere bundles of tropes. We find that the view that the link between such a bundle and an individual trope in the bundle – which is the bundle theory's account of the link between a particular and one of its properties – may still be accounted a necessary one. One who so accounts it is Peter Simons.[4] And indeed, any bundle theory, whether bundle of tropes or bundle of universals, seems to push towards the necessity of predication where members of the bundle are concerned. Predication of the member is a mere matter of extracting the trope or the universal from the bundle. (Compare: *a* is a member of the class $\{a, b, c, \dots\}$.)

4.4. UNIVERSALS AND INSTANTIATION

I have had a change of heart about the instantiation of universals. In previous work I conceived of the instantiation as a matter of contingent

---

[4] Simons, in a personal communication, tells me that, although he holds to non-transferability, and thinks that there are premises in his work from which it follows, he has nowhere in his published work set out the argument.

connection of particulars with universals. New work by Donald Baxter, at the University of Connecticut, has made me think that the link is necessary. See his paper 'Instantiation as partial identity' (2001). I have been convinced by him that what is involved in a particular instantiating a property-universal is a *partial identity* of the particular and universal involved. It is not a mere mereological overlap, as when two streets intersect, but it is a partial identity. This in turn has led me to hold that instantiation is not contingent but necessary.

I should make it clear, however, that he and I do not agree on the *necessity* of the substance-attribute distinction. Baxter says that although his proposal involves the intersection or partial identity of particulars and universals, he nevertheless holds that their relation is contingent. (See his 2001, pp. 449 and 462.)

The issue is difficult, but I think that this part of Baxter's position is wrong. (I argue the matter in more detail in my 'How do particulars stand to universals?' (Armstrong, 2004).) What is contingent might not have existed. Suppose *a* to be F, with F a universal. If this state of affairs is contingent, then it might not have existed. Suppose it had not existed. The particular *a*, the particular with all its non-relational properties, what I have in the past called the 'thick particular', would not then have existed. Something quite like it could have existed instead: a particular with all of *a*'s properties except F. But that would have been only a *close counterpart* of *a*, because the intersection with F, the partial identity with F, would be lacking. *Equally, it now seems to me, the universal F would not have existed.*[5] A universal very like F could have existed: a universal that had the same instantiations as F except for its instantiating *a*. But that would have only been a close counterpart of F, because the intersection with *a*, the partial identity with *a*, would not have existed. So, strictly, if *a* and F exist, then they *must* 'intersect'. They themselves can be, and I think are, contingent beings. But if *a* exists and F exists, then *a* must be F: a necessary connection between contingent beings.[6]

[5] This is the point that Baxter would object to.
[6] Hume denied necessary connections between distinct existences. Wholes and their proper parts, and also overlapping entities, are *different* from each other and so are, in some clear sense, distinct from each other. Hume, I take it, was not concerned to deny necessary connection in such cases. He wanted to deny necessary connection between *wholly* distinct existences. It is interesting to note, then, that partial identity of a particular and its universal does not contravene the Humean principle when it is restricted to wholly distinct existences.

I think that the view is best presented, in classical fashion, as two 'ones over many' or, even better, as two 'ones running through many'. Properties (the sparse properties) are, for Aristotelian realism about universals, ones that run through a plurality of particulars. Different particulars can have the very same property. But we also need the conception of particulars as ones that run through a plurality of universals. Different properties can all attach to the very same particular. Given this conception, which can be represented as a table with the different particulars as the columns and the different universals as the rows, it can be seen that *a particular's having a property* becomes an intersection of column and row.

I re-emphasize that such a theory can supply a *substitute* for contingency by offering counterparts. That *a* is F is necessary, but contingent *a* might not have existed and an *a*-like object that is not *a* might have existed that is not F. The situation is much the same as David Lewis's counterpart theory. For Lewis, an *a* that is an F strictly cannot exist in 'another possible world' without property F. All that can exist in the other world is a more or less close counterpart of *a*. He seems to be prepared to call this 'contingency', but it is a contingency in only a *loose* sense. Strictly, I think, he is (or he should be) a *necessitarian* about predication. Notice that counterpart theory is available even to one who denies the hypothesis of many possible worlds, provided that this-worldly truthmakers for truths of possibility can be found. (See ch. 6 for my attempt to provide such truthmakers.)

If this new theory of how particulars stand to universals is correct, then the necessity involved seems to change the situation in looking for truthmakers in a number of controversial fields, for instance the status of laws of nature. It also involves rethinking the matter of states of affairs.

4.5. STATES OF AFFAIRS

But let us begin by going back to theories that make the connection between particulars and properties contingent. It does not matter whether we work with tropes or universals, and again whether we work with bundles or substances with attributes. The same powerful truthmaker argument for states of affairs or (metaphysical) facts can be mounted. We have somehow got to get particulars and their properties together, or else somehow get the bundles tied up. Since the links needed are contingent (I am assuming for the moment), the entities to be linked cannot do the job by themselves. Truthmakers must necessitate, and the mere entities or their mere mereological sum by hypothesis cannot necessitate the linkages required. So there must exist states of affairs to be the truthmakers, to get us beyond the 'loose and separate' entities. The states of affairs may be bundlings of tropes, or attachments of tropes to particulars, or bundlings of universals ('compresence'), or instantiations of universals. States of affairs must be introduced *as additions to the ontology*.

The situation is different where the possession of properties by particulars is taken to be necessary. Consider first the Martin–Heil view where property-tropes are non-transferable, even as a mere possibility, from the particulars they qualify. There is no need for states of affairs *as an ontological extra*. This should not, I think, lead to denying that there are states of affairs. After all, they are needed to act as truthmakers for predicative truths. While *a* + trope F can be said to be the truthmaker for *a* is F, this is only because F is non-transferably linked to *a*. Supposing *a* not to be G, but G-type tropes to be found elsewhere, then the mereological sum *a* + G exists, but it does not yield a state of affairs involving *a* because a link between *a* and G is lacking.

The situation is the same if we turn to the theory I now incline to: *a*'s being F being necessary because *a* and universal F intersect, and are thus partially identical. Given *a* and given F, as opposed to mere counterparts of this particular and this universal, then the state of affairs of *a*'s being F is automatically there. It is built into the two constituents of the state of affairs. I would hope to extend the partial identity theory to cover relations as well as properties in the strict or monadic sense, but that development of the theory will not be discussed here.

It is important to observe that making <*a* is F> a necessary truth does not make the state of affairs *a*'s being F a necessary existent. That would follow only if *a* and F were necessary beings. Such a Spinozistic view can perhaps be held. Appearances of contingency would then have to be construed as the product of ignorance. The truthmaker for <*a* is F> would then indeed be a necessary state of affairs. But the view that I should like at present to champion is that *a* and F are necessarily connected but are themselves contingent beings. They might not have existed. If they might not have existed, then *a*'s being F might not have existed, and so this state of affairs is a contingent being. The ordinary ways contemporary philosophers use to argue for this contingency fail, as I now think. It is no good to suggest that *a* might have existed but not be F. The best that might have existed is a counterpart of *a*. But the state of affairs that is the truthmaker for <*a* is F> remains a contingent being.

4.6. RELATIONS

Some cursory attention has already been given to the topic of relations in this chapter, but more needs to be said. What truthmakers should we postulate as truthmakers for truths that certain objects stand in certain relations to other objects? To begin the enquiry, will the mere related objects, the mereological sum of these objects perhaps, serve as truthmakers for the truth that they stand in a certain relation? For certain relations this seems to be the case. Consider the truth <Venus is a different entity from Mars> (I mean the planets in each case). For this truth, Venus + Mars would appear to be a minimal truthmaker, indeed a unique minimal truthmaker. The same goes for the relation of difference that holds between circularity and squareness. The latter two entities, whatever we take the metaphysics of properties to be, seem to be unique minimal truthmakers for the holding of the relation. Consider, now, the truth <Venus is greater in size than Mars>, and let us assume, for the sake of argument, that size is a non-relational property of particulars. Venus + Mars seems to be still a truthmaker for this truth, but it is not clear that it is a *minimal* truthmaker. For this truth, it seems that we do not need all the properties of the two objects, or even all their non-relational properties. It is enough that Venus is a certain particular size, and that Mars is a certain particular size. These are states of affairs. The minimal truthmaker appears to be the mereological sum of these two states of affairs. The other properties of Venus and Mars seem irrelevant.

These two relations of *difference* and *greater in size than* are internal, a notion that has already been introduced and used at various points in the argument. I define it as one where the terms of the relation (or perhaps just some of the terms) necessitate the presence of the relation. My contention is that the terms, by themselves, can serve as truthmaker for the truth that the relation holds. The relation is no 'addition of being' to the terms. If this is correct, then here we have cases where the form of the *truth*: <*a* has R to *b*>, fails to reflect the nature of the reality, the truthmaker, that makes it true because the truthmaker is no more than *a* + *b*. In particular, states of affairs are not needed. A somewhat *deflationary* truthmaker is thus being offered for this sort of truth.

Two points. First, since the truthmaker necessitates its truth, the truthmaking relation is itself an internal one. So it will demand only the truthmaker and the true proposition it makes true. The ontological cost, therefore, of the truthmaker theory itself is not particularly onerous, though we do need a satisfactory theory of propositions (first discussed at 2.6).

The account of the ontology of internal relations can, of course, be resisted. One can then link the two states of affairs of *Venus being a certain size* and *Mars being a certain size* by the necessary state of affairs that the first of these sizes is greater than the second. But for myself, I hope to get by without such truthmakers. As indicated in 4.3, I now have sympathy with the view that predications are necessary truths. Once given their constituents, states of affairs will be necessary, not contingent. But this does not force one to postulate extra necessary states of affairs in connection with *internal* relations. In the case given, the two states of affairs involving Venus and Mars will suffice as truthmakers for the internal relation between their sizes.

We turn now from internal to external relations. These are, as it were, the true relations, polyadic properties, really existing in the world. The same arguments used in the case of the monadic properties make it plausible that there are such entities. If it is true that at a certain time Venus is a certain distance from Mars, an account in terms of polyadic predicates, ordered classes or resemblances between this and other situations shows little promise of providing satisfactory truthmakers. We need genuine relations, I think, whether universals or tropes, and, once again, these relations will be embedded in polyadic states of affairs.

Again, we should not expect that there is any one-one or other neat correlation between polyadic predicates, on the one hand, and the true and objective relations, on the other. What the latter are must be established *a posteriori* just as in the case of properties.

In the case of relations, however, it seems possible for philosophers to contribute directly to the discussion of what major classes of external relations that there are. The discussion, as far as I know, was begun by Hume in the *Treatise* (bk. I, pt. i, sec. 5 and pt. ii, secs. 1 and 2). It is, indeed, one of the finest things that Hume did in metaphysics. What we now call internal relations he speaks of as 'relations of ideas', and he has no term for the external relations. But he thinks that the latter are confined to spatiotemporal relations and causality. He does also list 'identity', but he means by that identity over time, and this identity he thinks of in Joseph Butler's terms as 'loose and popular' or in his own more coat-trailing terms as 'feigned'. He goes on to argue that this 'identity' can be analysed in terms of spatiotemporal relations and causality, the latter being particularly important in his analysis.

Even if these sorts of relation are not the only external relations, still they do have strong claims to be external. Strong claims, but in the case of causality the externality may be disputed. Suppose that one thinks of properties as causal powers, and suppose further that they are deterministic powers, powers that, in the right conditions, must bring about their effect. Then, where the conditions are right, the effect follows from the cause with absolute necessity. This, however, makes the causal relation an internal relation according to our definition of internal relations. One might even say that the effect would be supervenient upon the cause. But it could hardly be a supervenience where what supervenes is no addition of being. Cause and effect must surely be distinct existences even if they are necessarily connected, and so the effect must be an addition of being. We would have in such a case a necessary connection between these distinct existences. Or putting it in terms of truthmakers, the truthmakers for such causal truths will involve a necessary connection *in re*. (Causality, together with laws, will be the subject of chapter 10. I do not myself hold the view that properties are causal powers, although I think it is a very interesting theory to consider.)

One point that may be noted about states of affairs is that, if a trope theory is accepted for properties, then subject/attribute theories, theories that involve irreducible particularity, seem to handle polyadic states of affairs a little more easily than the more popular bundle theories. Just as in theories of relation-universals, a single external relation binds up a plurality of particulars into a state of affairs. And if non-transferability works for the monadic case, it seems little different when extended to polyadic cases. But suppose that two particulars, the earth and the moon say, are mere bundles of tropes. What does the external relation of distance, say, hold between? If, as seems natural, it holds between the two bundles, each taken as a whole, then since each bundle is a complex state of affairs, the relation will become a higher-order state of affairs holding between the two very complex states of affairs.

In the past I have regarded external relations as holding contingently only, and I think that this has been the assumption generally made. But as noted in 4.5, this assumption can be questioned. Whether such relations are considered to be universals, or instead considered to be tropes, perhaps they should be thought of as necessary. We can then, I think, still distinguish internal from external relations because the external relations demand states of affairs while the internal relations do not.

5

Negative truths

Chapters 5 and 6, on truthmakers for negative truths and general truths, were originally conceived of as one chapter, because the two topics are closely linked. They have been separated to make it easier for the reader. I would also like to call attention to the penultimate section of chapter 6: 'New thinking about general facts'. It puts forward a rather different line to that taken in the rest of the two chapters, one that depends on taking the instantiation of universals by particulars as a matter of partial identity, a matter already canvassed in 4.3 and 4.4. It involves important changes in my view on a number of matters.

Problems about not-being have been with philosophy since the time of Parmenides, at least. They constitute some of the most difficult problems in the discipline of metaphysics. Within truthmaking theory they appear as the question what truthmakers we are to provide for truths of non-existence, for instance the truths that centaurs and unicorns do not exist, and all the true denials that things that do exist have certain (positive) properties or relations, for instance the lack of whiteness of certain swans. We also need to extend the enquiry to general truths, for instance the truths that all men are mortal or all ravens are black. For these, too, are a species of negative truth, 'no more' truths, asserting that there are no more men than the mortal ones, no more ravens than the black ones. We may distinguish between *absences* and *limits*. There is an absence of unicorns, or an absence of whiteness in the case of a certain swan. That these are *all* the persons in a certain room at a certain time sets a limit to persons in the room at that time.

It seems to me that, even among the select and virtuous band that have embraced truthmaking theory, most have a rather sorry record in their discussions of these problems. A great many have denied, as I believe that they should not have denied, that truthmakers, or at any rate necessitating truthmakers, can be found for these truths. The glorious exception is Russell, in his *Logical Atomism* lectures (Russell, 1972). Besides his atomic facts he argues for existential facts, negative facts and general facts. (Indeed, I shall argue shortly that he overdoes things somewhat.)

An important point here may be that Russell is one of the relatively few philosophers who is definitely committed to a Factualist ontology, as opposed to a Thingist (Reist) view. If you hold, or presuppose in your thinking without making it explicit – perhaps even to yourself – that the world is a world of things rather than a world of facts (states of affairs, as I prefer to say), then negative truths are a very great difficulty. You can point to the actually existing things, but then there seems nothing more to point to. One may speculate that the view of the courageous Meinong that the non-existent ought to be (in some sense!) included in one's ontology is an attempt to deal with the problem of negative truth, but within a Thingist framework of thought. As a Factualist, I am hoping to accommodate negative truths more plausibly than Meinong did.

5.2. CAN WE DISPENSE WITH NEGATIVE FACTS?

In the *Logical Atomism* lectures, Russell recognizes, in addition to atomic facts (the truthmakers for true atomic propositions), existential facts, negative facts and general facts. He draws the line at disjunctive facts, for obvious reasons. All that is required for them is a truthmaker for at least one disjunct, and then there seems no need to postulate disjunctive facts in addition. The question is whether Russell was not too generous here. It is not difficult to argue that existential facts are not really required. I concede, indeed propose to argue, following Russell, that general facts are required (at any rate given that they are contingent). But I will argue in addition that provided we allow ourselves general facts then no *further* negative facts are needed among our truthmakers.[1]

Existential facts, the fact that there exist horses and so on, appear to supervene in an unproblematic manner upon monadic and polyadic facts (states of affairs). Why postulate in addition to these facts a special sort of

---

[1] It is generally assumed that in the *Tractatus* (1961) Wittgenstein denied the need for general facts. I suppose that this derives from 4.0312: 'My fundamental thought is that the logical constants do not represent.' But John Heil has drawn my attention to 1.11: 'The world is determined by the facts and by these being *all* the facts' [Wittgenstein's italics]. Was this part of the ladder to be thrown away at the end?

state of affairs: that at least one horse exists? All those monadic and polyadic states of affairs that involve horses would seem to be perfectly satisfactory truthmakers for the truth that at least one horse exists. Thus, it is true that <the horse Old Rowley once won the Melbourne Cup>. This truth is made true by a complex polyadic state of affairs. Given the omnitemporal reading of the existential quantifier (which will be argued for in ch. 9) the truth entails that <at least one horse exists>. Using the Entailment principle (2.5) in what seems to be a legitimate context here, it follows that the truthmaker for this truth about Old Rowley is the truthmaker for the truth that <at least one horse exists>. No special truthmaker is required for the existential truth. *Minimal* (or at least close to minimal) truthmakers for this existential truth will be each individual horse. It will be seen that here we have a case where a truth has many minimal truthmakers.

So we can move on to the serious ontological problem: truthmakers for negative truths. In the first place I assume that there is an ontological distinction to be drawn between predicates that apply in virtue of properties and those that apply in virtue of their absence. There are difficult cases, no doubt, but one should look to science rather than grammar to determine disputed cases. Any first-order particular will have a great number of positive properties. For these, first-order facts (states of affairs) would seem to be adequate truthmakers. But it is also true that the particular will *lack* an indefinite number of properties. What sort of truthmakers are we to supply for these? Should we credit the particular with negative properties: *not being a kilogram in mass*, and so on for all the other masses or other properties that it does not happen to have? This would seem to be enormously uneconomical, particularly because it is hard to credit these putative properties with causal efficacy. This in turn makes it hard to see how we can get knowledge or rational belief of their existence. Or should we introduce negative states of affairs: *its not being the case that this particular has a mass of one kilogram*? This seems only a little better.

A position that a number of truthmaker theorists take is that we do not need truthmakers for negative truths. Such truths, they say, do not have falsemakers, and this is all that we can say about them. But to say this is in fact to say very little. Of course negative truths do not have falsemakers. No truth has a falsemaker, whether it be negative or positive! So to say that negative truths do not have falsemakers is, in this context, really to say no more than to say that negative truths lack truthmakers. But why should one who accepts truthmakers baulk at truthmakers for negative truth? Are we not giving up when the ontological going gets a bit tough?

How might we improve? Begin at the level of truths rather than truth-makers. Consider the truth that <Theaetetus is not flying>. Theaetetus has all sorts of positive properties. (We are talking about him at the time of his conversation with Socrates, as reported or imagined by Plato in the *Sophist*.) For instance, he is sitting and he has, like Socrates, a snub nose. But now let us, in imagination, make out a long list of all the positive properties predicable of Theaetetus at that time. We do not want to go on and make out a still longer list of all the properties that he lacks. Is it possible to avoid this?

We can begin by following Plato and noting that each property that Theaetetus has not got, of which flying is an instance, is *different* from any of his actual properties. This is a very important insight, because difference is an objective relation that holds between entities that actually exist (birds fly, so there is a property of flying). What is more, the truthmaker for the truth that one entity is different from another entity seems to be nothing more than the two entities themselves. (Just as the truthmaker for the truth that an object is identical with itself is nothing more than the object.) Posit the entities and you have their difference. One by one, we can say that Theaetetus' positive properties are different from the property of flying.

Can we leave the matter here? Can we say that it is the totality of Theaetetus' actual properties (strictly, the conjunction of the states of affairs that involve the man and his properties) that are the truthmakers for <Theaetetus is not flying>? (It may be urged, differently, that Theaetetus may well have certain properties that are incompatible with flying. Perhaps this is the case with the property of sitting, for instance. But I want to leave this point aside for the moment. I will consider the interesting Incompatibility solution independently at 5.2.1.) If we forget about incompatibilities for the moment, it seems that Theaetetus' having positive properties F, G, H, . . . might be enough as truthmaker for each negative truth about Theaetetus. After all, this class of properties is coextensive with *all* of Theaetetus' positive properties, and any other suggested positive property is different from these properties. So Theaetetus would lack the suggested property.

I do indeed think that the conjunction of states of affairs that exhausts Theaetetus' positive properties is a necessary part of the truthmaker for <Theaetetus is not flying>. But I think it is a proper part only. The trouble is that the big conjunction, as we may call it, when taken by itself fails to *necessitate* <Theaetetus is not flying>. The big conjunction could exist and yet Theaetetus be flying. (Assuming, as we are assuming here, that his positive properties and his flying are compatible.) This can be concealed if we talk of the *class* of Theaetetus' positive properties. If we speak of the class of Fs, we intend all the Fs. But if we simply take the class 'in extension', as it were running through a list, then although it be in fact all the Fs, it may not be necessarily all the Fs. In the same way, the big conjunction does not exhaust Theaetetus' positive properties *of necessity*.

Perhaps one could simply drop the condition that the truthmaker for a negative truth should necessitate that truth. I find myself unable in conscience to take this path. Truthmakers that fail to necessitate, it seems to me, leave something out. So I look for an additional element to add to the big conjunction to produce a necessitating truthmaker. And so, in looking for truthmakers for *not*, I find myself looking for truthmakers for *all*. If we had, in addition to the list, the truthmaker for <this is the conjunction of all Theaetetus' positive properties> then, it seems, we would have a necessitating truthmaker for <Theaetetus is not flying>.

It is not clear whether Plato actually reached this point. He emphasizes that the property of flying (a real property, really possessed by certain things) is a *different* property from the property of sitting or being snub-nosed. Whether he wished explicitly to bring in the universal quantifier, to point to the fact that flying was different from *all* of Theaetetus' actual properties, is not so clear, though his words perhaps can be so read. In Russell's Introduction to *Principia Mathematica*, however, a line of thought of the same general sort becomes more or less explicit:

Given all true atomic propositions,[2] together with the fact that they are all, every other true proposition can theoretically be deduced by logical methods. That is to say, the apparatus of crude fact required in proofs can all be condensed into the true atomic propositions together with the fact that every true atomic proposition is one of the following: (here the list should follow). If used, this method would presumably involve an infinite enumeration, since it seems natural to suppose that the number of true atomic propositions is infinite, though this should not be regarded as certain. In practice, generality is not obtained by the method of complete enumeration, because this method requires more knowledge than we possess.[3]

Here Russell has argued for a certain entailment. It is not a difficult task, and one already largely indicated, to adapt this insight to the purposes of truthmaker theory. Assume that to each true atomic proposition corresponds its own atomic fact (atomic state of affairs). Consider then the

---

[2] Note that these are all supposed to be positive.
[3] Russell and Whitehead, 1968, p. xv. I thank Herbert Hochberg for the reference.

proposition that conjoins all these propositions and asserts <this conjunction is the totality of true atomic propositions> (the conjunction may be infinite). It does appear that this huge, and apparently contingent, proposition entails all the contingent negative truths and also all lesser truths of totality such as the truth that a certain list of properties is the totality of, say, Theaetetus' properties. So, using the Entailment principle once again, any truthmaker for the huge proposition will be a truthmaker (generally not a minimal truthmaker) for all contingent negative truths, including both internal and external negations.

Returning to Theaetetus, what is the truthmaker for the truth <Theaetetus is not flying> on this analysis? There is a certain conjunction of first-order states of affairs in which Theaetetus figures. These, we assert, involve nothing but positive properties. (Relational properties can be included, but they too must all be positive.) Postulate a further, higher-order state of affairs: that this collection is *all* the states of affairs in which Theaetetus is involved. Is this not a good candidate for a truthmaker for the negative truth? (It may not be a minimal truthmaker. Perhaps for a minimal truthmaker for <Theaetetus is not flying> we need only collect, among the states of affairs that have Theaetetus as a constituent, those that involve his positive states of motion and rest. But we are leaving the Incompatibility solution aside for the present.)

Here we have *not* got away completely from negative states of affairs. The *all* state of affairs is itself a 'no more' state of affairs, setting a limit to the states of affairs that involve Theaetetus, and so setting a limit to his properties. But a very great ontological economy has been effected. We get rid of the ontological nightmare of either a huge number of negative properties or a huge number of negative states of affairs, and substitute for them a single *all* state of affairs. It is a state of affairs (admittedly, a pretty large state of affairs, subsuming innumerable lesser allnesses), one that will serve as a truthmaker for the huge number of negative *truths* about Theaetetus among other particulars.

It is true that the suggested truthmaker is a higher-order state of affairs, and as a result those in love with the *Tractatus* vision of nothing but a single level of facts or states of affairs may see this as a serious lack of economy. But I contend, with Russell, that 'general facts' (totality states of affairs, as I like to put it) have to be introduced in any case. If that is correct, we should use them as truthmakers for all the other negative truths. They have to be there. So let them really earn their keep! Here, of course, I am departing from the view defended by Russell in the *Logical Atomism* lectures. In those lectures he argues, a little hesitantly, for negative facts, and without any hesitation at all for general facts, but, a little strangely in view of the passage just quoted from the Introduction to *Principia*, he makes no attempt to bring the two topics together. (The *Principia* passage, however, was written some years after the lectures.)

I am by no means claiming to have *conclusively* ruled out extra, first-order but negative states of affairs. It remains possible to argue that we should recognize both the general facts and also the other negative facts. But the existence of the positive first-order facts plus the existence of the general fact that collects them will entail the corresponding negative first-order facts. This entailment at least suggests that the first-order negatives are not needed in our ontology. Putting it colourfully, if God decrees a certain body of first-order positive states of affairs and then decrees that these are enough, there seems no need for him to establish first-order negative properties or states of affairs *in addition*. The first-order negative properties can certainly be said to be real. It is a *fact* in the ordinary sense of the word 'fact' that this swan on the Swan river in West Australia is not white-plumaged. But such facts seem to be no addition of being to general states of affairs.

Advancing beyond the case of Theaetetus, we can see, as Russell seems to see in the recently quoted passage, that there is a huge general fact (state of affairs) that is the most general state of affairs of all. It is, it would seem, a contingent state of affairs. The world might have been bigger than it actually is. So, by the Entailment principle, the great general state of affairs is a truthmaker for all the other negative truths about particulars. A metaphysician could still maintain that these negative truths had additional truthmakers besides. But what motive is there for this?

These arguments might be thrown into uncertainty if the first-order positives plus the first-order *negatives* were sufficient to necessitate the general facts. But this seems not to be so. The situation is asymmetrical. Suppose, for instance, a small world with only two atomic particulars, each with just one property, F for *a*, G for *b*. Put negative properties into the ontology, *a* having property *not-G*, and *b* having property *not-F*. Add as many further first-order negative properties to each particular as you please. How are you going to exclude the possibility that *a* and *b* have further positive properties? Only, it seems, if the negative properties plus the positive properties of *a* and *b* *exhaust* the properties of these objects. But how is this condition to be given a necessitating truthmaker without a higher-order fact that these first-order negative properties plus the actual positive properties are *all* the properties of the objects? At that point, it seems far more economical to go back to the original solution, which deals in positive properties alone, and the fact (state of affairs) that puts a closure on these positives.

5.2.1. *The Incompatibility solution*

If one wants to avoid negative and/or general states of affairs as truthmakers, one will be attracted to the idea that, given the existence of certain positive entities, certain negative states of affairs are necessarily excluded. Given an object that is square, it cannot be that that object is circular. Given a surface that is red, it cannot be that it is green. One might embrace hopes of generalizing this solution to deal with all negative truths. The view seems to have been first articulated by Raphael Demos, who attended that famous class at Harvard where Russell's championing of negative facts was said by Russell to have 'nearly produced a riot' (Demos, 1917; Russell, 1972, p. 67).

The general form of this solution is the claim that for every negative truth $\neg q$ there exists a positive truth p that is incompatible with q. (Demos himself restricts his claim somewhat.) The truth that p will have a straightforward truthmaker. By the Entailment principle (valid in general, at least) this will also be a truthmaker for $\neg q$.

Perhaps this case can be strengthened by bringing in Peter Simons's insight concerning incompatibilities (see 2.4). Consider the proposition of the form $<x$ is incompatible with $y>$ from the standpoint of truthmaker theory. Take it that p is true (so it has truthmakers), and is incompatible with q. These same truthmakers will be falsemakers for q. A falsemaker for q is automatically a truthmaker for $\neg q$. That seems to be all that a truthmaker version of the Incompatibility theory need say.

It was objected by Russell (1972, pp. 69–70), and the objection has been repeated by others, that a truth of incompatibility is itself a negative truth. It is also, however, a necessary truth. It was pointed out by the late George Molnar, however (Molnar, 2000, pp. 74–5), that if, as do many who accept truthmakers, one holds that all necessary truths lack or have trivial truthmakers, Russell's objection will not be a difficulty. Molnar, himself did not accept this view of necessary truths. He thought that proper truthmakers should be found for them, although I do not know what his account would have been. I will be proposing serious truthmakers for all modal truths in chapters 7 and 8, but in my account of modal truths negative modal truths do not seem to involve any particular complication. As a result, I do not think that this objection to the Incompatibility view is a serious one.

If one holds a *power* theory of properties, identifying properties with the powers that they bestow on their particulars, then (as most power theorists agree) physical incompatibilities will at the same time be metaphysical incompatibilities, that is, necessary incompatibilities. (Molnar himself held just such a theory.) This will greatly improve the prospects of an Incompatibility theory. A wide range of negative truths can then be argued to be incompatibilities with the actual physical situation.

Of course, if one rejects the power theory and one also takes the laws of nature to be contingent, then the task of an Incompatibility theorist becomes somewhat harder. A further matter that may make difficulty for the Incompatibility theory is that what pass for mere attributions of properties often include covertly a general fact. It is sometimes this general fact that is setting up the incompatibility rather than the property itself. Consider 'He is six feet tall.' The state of affairs that makes this truth true might be thought to rule out his having both greater and lesser heights. The lesser heights are indeed ruled out. But it seems, however, that the greater heights are ruled out only because what is asserted is ordinarily taken to be 'He is six feet tall *and no more.*' The six feet are *all* that he has in the way of height. The statement has a covert totality clause tacked on.

(Consider by way of contrast being asked if one has five dollars immediately available to lend, and saying that one does. Let it be the case that one actually has twenty dollars on hand. In most ordinary circumstances, the fact of having the twenty dollars is not taken to make it false that one has five dollars. Having five dollars, and having five dollars *and no more*, are not necessarily the same thing.)

Another case has been brought to my attention by John Bigelow. Consider the methane molecule, with its carbon atom at the centre and four hydrogen atoms bonded to this atom. Does the existence of these five atoms, suitably bonded, yield a methane molecule? It seems not. For consider the possibility of a larger molecule containing *as a proper part* the atoms that make up a methane molecule bonded just as they are within the methane molecule. (I do not know whether this is chemically possible, so I speak under correction from chemists.) It would seem that this is not a methane molecule. To be a methane molecule, it must contain five suitable atoms, four hydrogen and one carbon suitably bonded, and, furthermore, that must be *all* the atoms that it contains. So, being a methane molecule only excludes the larger molecules envisaged because a totality state of affairs is included in the concept of methane.

It is also interesting to note that if we speak of the *class* of the Xs, then, as already noted earlier in this essay, we are speaking of *all* the Xs. The concept of *the class of Xs* has totality built into it. These factors all make the Incompatibility theorist's task somewhat harder because the exclusions of negative states of affairs must be by the positive properties alone and not by any concealed totality condition.

Nevertheless, the Incompatibility solution to the problem of truthmakers for negative truths clearly has something going for it. This is shown by the difficulty there is in finding examples of negative truths where a plausible Incompatibilist solution cannot be found. Molnar, who rejects Incompatibilism, suggests that there are *purely accidental negatives*. He gives as an example a particular atom in a pile of radium atoms that is *not* in a decay state (2000, p. 75). This example, I take it, depends on the assumption that a particular atom not being in a decay state is a purely probabilistic matter, and one unaffected by the other radium atoms present. There is then, Molnar suggests, no positive property of the atom for the Incompatibilist to point to that is incompatible with the atom not being in a decay state. Assuming that this is the true physics of the matter, the example seems to succeed. But it is important to notice that Molnar goes to high-level scientific theory – which may be later overthrown – to find his counter-example.

But perhaps more mundane examples can be found. Consider the traditional and useful contrast that philosophers make between determinable and determinate properties. Length is a determinable, being some particular length, such as a mile, is one of its determinates. Colour is a determinable, scarlet is one of its determinates. As is well known, a huge number of properties (and also many relations and even functional laws of nature) can be regimented under this scheme. *Determinates* are where the Incompatibilist triumphs. A set of determinates under the one determinable are incompatible by definition. If an object is not a mile in length, then in normal cases at least, it will be some other length, a length incompatible with being a mile in length. If an object is not scarlet, this will be because it is some other definite colour, a colour incompatible with being scarlet.

Surrendering determinates that fall under the same determinable to the Incompatibilist, let us consider determinables. The simplest cases will be the so-called secondary qualities. What of contingent, negative, and true propositions such as <this has no smell>, <this has no taste>, <this is

62

colourless>, <this is making no sound>? What positive properties of the object can be found that exclude these things of necessity? If the laws of nature are necessary, then perhaps it can be argued that these negative propositions are necessitated by whatever causes the object to lack the determinate in question. But if the laws are contingent, then the Incompatibilist may seem to have no solution for these cases.

It may be objected on behalf of the Incompatibilist that given a certain theory of the secondary qualities (one that I myself subscribe to), his situation is still not hopeless. If a physicalist theory of the secondary qualities is correct, then these qualities reduce to micro-physical primary properties, and then there may well be something about the actual, positive, physical properties of the object that necessitates (a non-propositional necessity) that it lacks the secondary quality in question.

At this point, however, we come to what I think is a good reason to reject the Incompatibility theory. The trouble with the theory is that its truth or falsity seems to depend far too much on the way that the world happens to be. Should not our account of negation, an all-pervasive and fundamental feature of our thought and discourse, be such as to demand truthmakers that do not depend upon the particular way that the world happens to be? This demand, I think, is met by the solution in terms of general facts, *allness* states of affairs. We have to have such truthmakers – we would have to have them in any world. They do the job, it seems, for all other negative truths. So, although the Incompatibilist position is an interesting one, one that may even be extensionally equivalent, or very nearly equivalent, to the solution in terms of general facts, I do not think that we should accept it.

5.2.2. *Preventions, omissions and the Deadly Void*

One argument for negative states of affairs additional to totality states of affairs should now be considered. We do speak, and appear to speak truly, of omissions, lacks and absences as *causes*. A man omits to take sufficient water into the Outback. *As a result*, he does a perish, to use the idiom of the locals. Lack of water caused his death. You are absent from a vital meeting. *As a result*, a decision is made that you do not want made, and could have prevented. Your absence was the cause of the meeting going the wrong way. So omissions appear to be causes. By contrast, preventing is, generally at least, a positive thing. You catch the child who is about to run into the road and be run down by a car. But here the effect, what is prevented, is, generally at least, that something that would, or might, have happened but, as a result of the preventing event, *does not happen*. The effect is something negative, the non-happening of something. Do we not need negative states of affairs for these negative effects and negative causes?

I think that this is ontologically mistaken. All singular causes and effects, *strictly so called*, are, I maintain, positive states of affairs. When we speak of causes and effects in connection with omissions, lacks, absences and preventions, the truthmakers involved, if what we say is true, are certain positive causal processes *plus* the truthmakers for certain sorts of *counterfactuals*, counterfactuals involving causality. I owe this insight to Phil Dowe (see his 2000, ch. 6). The counterfactuals needed I call Dowe counterfactuals. These counterfactuals are emphatically not the counterfactuals that David Lewis has made us familiar with in his counterfactual theory of causality. Lewis is trying to analyse singular causality. The Dowe counterfactuals leave singular causation as an unanalysed primitive. They are, indeed, as Dowe points out in detail, compatible with the great majority of *theories* of the nature of singular causation. Dowe's counterfactuals make almost no stand on the question what are the truthmakers for truths involving singular causation. That is their strength.

Consider prevention first. There is always causal action. A foot is stamped on a brake, and as a result the car is slowed. These are positive happenings. There is also a counterfactual: if the braking had not occurred, then the *un*slowed car would have caused, say, a nasty collision. Now consider omission. Causal processes within a live human being deprived of water fairly quickly bring it about that the person becomes dead. That latter condition is here negatively described, but it is nevertheless a positive physiological condition. The counterfactual truth is <if the body had received water, that water would have *enabled* the body [enabling is a causal notion] to continue in the living state>. There are more complex cases than these, omissions of preventions, preventions of omissions, preventions of preventions, but the same general pattern can be found.

Dowe has used billiard-table examples. As he and Hume before him realize, they provide simple, clear-cut examples to work with. Here is a prevention: a billiard ball, A, travels in a straight line towards billiard ball B. But A is prevented from causally affecting billiard ball B because ball C hits A first, deflecting it before A reaches B. Dowe emphasizes that in all cases of 'negative causation' there is some actual (positive) causality involved. Here it is C moving A from its original path. What makes this *prevention*?

All that need be added is a counterfactual, which here we may assume to be true, that <if C had not caused the deflection of A, then A would have hit B and caused it to move>. That is what this prevention *is*.

Suppose, instead, that ball C fails to hit ball A. This failure – a sort of omission – fails to prevent A hitting B. We have another counterfactual: <if C had indeed hit A, then A would have been prevented from hitting B>. The prevention again can be unpacked in the way indicated above.

Notice that we may not in practice know whether a causal sequence is in fact a case of prevention or not. Flipping a switch turns the light out. It takes a moment's thought, though, to realize that the causing is a matter of preventing the current from keeping the light burning. Opium causes sleep. But, as David Lewis pointed out to me, it might do this by blocking some process in the brain that would otherwise keep one awake. Opium might only be a preventer. Nevertheless, the distinction between straightforward causing and preventing is clear enough, even if we have not analysed the nature of the difference. Often, though, we do not *know* whether a particular sequence is one or the other. This ignorance, together with the fact that we are not always interested in whether a case is genuine causation or mere prevention or omission, helps to explain why we so easily run the ontologically different cases together in practice.

We still have to consider the question of the proper truthmakers for causal truths, an issue that must be postponed to a later chapter. But with causation taken as something unanalysed, it can be suggested that the truthmakers for the Dowe counterfactuals involved in the analysis of prevention and omission are the relevant causal laws (taken ontologically, not just as true propositions) plus the actual situation, the actual boundary conditions, that obtain in the particular case. (These boundary conditions may, of course, themselves include causal relations.) It is true that in the antecedent clause of causal conditionals we in imagination subtract the preventing event, or in imagination add some event in place of the omission. But that only concerns the 'semantics' of the conditionals. Unless we accept possible worlds among our truthmakers, which I am quite unwilling to do, it seems that the *truthmaker* for the counterfactual will be the ontological laws plus certain aspects of the situation as it actually is. It seems a satisfactory truthmaker.

If the argument of this section is correct, then it removes an important pressure to postulate first-order negative states of affairs in addition to totality states of affairs. We should perhaps take brief notice of the Deadly

Void. This is the case introduced by C. B. Martin (Martin, 1996). He imagines a void, something beyond a vacuum, genuine not-being, a real hole in being. It 'rolls' through the world apparently destroying what is in its path. But has it really got causal power? Martin himself says, 'Absences and voids are causally *relevant* but not causally *operative*' (p. 64). He does not spell out this gnomic but impressive statement, but presumably he would do so counterfactually in terms of what happens to objects in 'ordinary' environments. As David Lewis points out in 'Void and object' (Lewis, 2004), a vacuum kills a human being not because of anything it does to the human being but because of causal processes within the body. A body in a vacuum lacks the resources to sustain itself, so that processes go on within it that quickly lead to death. The 'effects' of the Deadly Void are no more than an extrapolation of the actual effects of the positive causal factors that operate in ordinary vacuums.

Absences and voids, then, need not be credited with causal powers. So an important pressure in favour of introducing negative states of affairs (or negative properties) is removed.

5.2.3. Preventions and omissions supervene

A further argument for treating causation involving prevention or omission as ontologically second-rate cases of causation is that they appear to supervene upon the cases where both cause and effect are positive states of affairs. (Call the latter cases the positive causations.) Now consider the totality of positive causations over the whole of space-time, plus the laws that govern these individual cases, the causal net as we may call it. Consider further the totality of preventions, omissions, preventions of preventions and so on, over the whole of space-time. (Call these the negative causations.) I do not claim to prove the proposition, but is it not very plausible that the negative causations supervene on the positive causations together with the laws that govern the positive causations?

Consider the billiard-ball cases discussed in 5.2.2. Ball A travels in a straight line and with some velocity towards ball B. However, A never hits B. At a certain point, ball C hits A and as a result A starts moving along a different line, a line that passes B by. This, it would seem, can all be spelt out in purely positive terms: the actual paths, velocities and actual momentums of the balls involved, paths that obey laws of motion. That C *prevented* A from hitting B seems not to be an extra state of affairs, but rather to supervene on the details of the positive causation. The truthmaker for

<C prevented A hitting B> seems to be found in the positive causes and their positive effects.

Suppose instead we have the situation where C does not hit A, but simply passes A by. A goes on and does hit B. Here we have what may be said to be a failure or omission of C to hit A, and so deflect A from hitting B. Again this seems to supervene on the positive causation, although actually calling it a failure or omission may hint at human objectives that were frustrated. The truthmaker for <C failed to prevent A hitting B> is once again purely positive.

5.2.4. Perception of absence

It may be useful to complete this discussion by considering the epistemology of negation. In particular, what account should we give of negative perception, for instance, looking into a room and 'seeing that there is nobody there'?

The situation is quite different from seeing a person in the room. In that case certain superficial parts of the person act on the eyes of the perceiver to produce the perception. But in the negative case it is the *absence* of any such action that cues the perceiver. It is as if the perceiver is reasoning from a conditional: if there were a person in the room then I would perceive them, but I am having no such perception, so there is nobody there. Perception of a negation, which includes perceptions of a totality ('I can see that they are all here'), has always an element of theory in it. In particular, it involves conditionals, and the truthmakers for these conditionals are of the same general sort that we have just been discussing. In these particular cases, it will be a matter of the perceptual powers of the one who perceives the absence. The truthmakers for these conditionals are to be spelt out in terms of boundary conditions – the state of the perceiver and environment – and the laws that govern such states.

We are not yet finished with negative truths, but we need at this point to turn our attention to that special species of negative truth: general truths.

6

General truths

6.1. TRUTHMAKERS FOR GENERAL TRUTHS

The idea being followed out is that if we have generality in the world –
general facts, totality states of affairs – then these will be satisfactory truthmakers for the *whole* class of negative truths, that is, the more obviously
negative truths plus the general truths. I here quote Russell in his defence
of general facts. He says:

I do not think one can doubt that there are general facts. It is perfectly clear, I
think, that when you have enumerated all the atomic facts in the world, it is a
further fact about the world that those are all the atomic facts there are about the
world, and that is just as much an objective fact about the world as any of them
are. It is clear, I think, that you must admit general facts as distinct from and over
and above particular facts. The same thing applies to 'All men are mortal'. When
you have taken all the particular men that there are, and found each one of them
severally to be mortal, it is definitely a new fact that all men are mortal; how new
a fact appears from what I said a moment ago, that it could not be inferred from
the mortality of the several men that there are in the world. (1972, pp. 93–4)

Here is a way of putting the argument. Take the mereological sum of
what happens to be all the men. It seems clear that this object does not
necessitate that it *is* all the men. So if truthmaking involves necessitation,
as I wish to maintain, then this object cannot be the complete truthmaker
for <these are all the men>.

Some philosophers who are to a degree sympathetic to the enterprise
of looking for truthmakers are nevertheless unsympathetic to Russell's position here. They include David Lewis and John Bigelow. They proceed
by trying to find a judicious weakening of the principle that every truth
should have a necessitating truthmaker. Falsemakers become very important for them. Certain truths are allowed to be true not because they have
truthmakers, but solely because they *lack falsemakers*. Thus, in Russell's case
of the totality of facts, what constitutes the totality of facts is, they say, just
this: the absence of any further facts. Lewis's own illustration is the truth

68

that no unicorns exist. This is made true by the absence of any unicorns in our world.

I have already pointed out the emptiness of saying that certain truths lack falsemakers. Every truth lacks a falsemaker! That is trivial. However, in his paper 'Truth-making and difference-making' (2001), Lewis has an ingenious formulation of the weakened principle he wishes to work with. He eventually modifies it still further to accommodate the absences of properties and relations. Here we will use his simpler preliminary formulation, but read 'something' so as to cover any sort of entity, including properties and relations:

(TM-) For any proposition P and any worlds W and V, if P is true in W but not in V, then either something exists in V but not in W or else something exists in W but not in V.

Suppose, for example, there are no unicorns in W, but there are unicorns in V. Let P be the proposition that unicorns do not exist. In W, P is true, true through lack of falsemakers. But in V, not-P is true, true in virtue of truthmakers. Lewis says:

Those otherworldly unicorns are the one-way difference makers between worlds like ours where the negative existential proposition that there are no unicorns is true and other worlds in which it is false; and in worlds where the negative existential proposition is false, they are the truthmakers for its true negation. What more do we need?

I agree with Lewis's final remark up to a point. Perhaps *he* does not need more. But this is because he has a metaphysics of really existing possible worlds and, furthermore, he makes these worlds all ontologically equal with each other. 'From its own point of view' each world exists, and the others are merely possible. Our world is no exception in Lewis's theory. It is not metaphysically privileged in this respect. Combine this with the observation that every positive and contingent existential proposition is true at some world, and so has truthmakers in the worlds in which it is true. The falsity of some particular positive existential proposition in *our* world, the non-existence of unicorns as it might be, is a local failing only. It is at least tempting, then, to economize on truthmakers at this point, and make do with an absence of falsemakers on the local scene. The falsemakers will not be absent in other worlds.

Suppose, however, that one holds, as I do and most of us do, that there is only one world, that 'our world' is the totality of being, and so must be that which makes every truth true. A Lewis-style analysis then becomes much less attractive for truthmaker theorists. Suppose that one is a one-worlder seeking the truthmaker for the negative existential truth that there are no unicorns. In this new context it is far less attractive to be told that it is merely the absence of falsemakers that 'makes' this sort of truth true. To try to analyse 'the absence of falsemakers' in terms of the unrealized possibility that the world might have been such that 'unicorns exist' is true seems ludicrous if it is *truthmakers* one is seeking. If one is a one-worlder, and one takes the truthmaking project seriously, it would seem that an absence of falsemakers is an *absence*. *Prima facie*, one has included absences – negative states of affairs – among one's truthmakers.

One can, of course, simply assert that a proposition such as <there are no unicorns> stands in no need of any truthmaker or other ontological ground. But this seems to be no more than giving up on truthmakers as soon as the going gets hard. My own suggestion, already advanced, is to follow the path at least adumbrated by Russell in the *Principia* and add nothing but general facts, totality states of affairs, to one's truthmakers. For instance, the totality of first-order positive states of affairs plus the higher-order state of affairs that these *are* all the first-order states of affairs necessitates the absences and lacks in the world. These general facts, because they set a limit, are themselves a species of negative fact. There is no getting away from negativity altogether. But general facts (states of affairs) seem at least to remove the need to postulate any *further* negative truthmakers.[1]

Lewis, however, offers some arguments against those who insist 'on positing some sort of truthmaker for the negative existential truth that there are no unicorns'. Following Lewis, call all such suggested truthmakers 'a unicorn replacement'. Such truthmakers, Lewis points out, must satisfy two conditions. If such a thing exists, it must necessitate the truth of the negative existential. And if the negative existential is true, there must be such a truthmaker. We might call it an 'absence of unicorns' or 'the negative state of affairs of there being no unicorns' or 'the general state of affairs of everything being a non-unicorn'. But all these truthmakers would be, he says, 'bad news for systematic metaphysics'. They are bad news because all these suggested truthmakers would involve 'necessary connections between (mereologically) distinct existences'.

---

[1] I should note that in my 1978, ch. 14, II, I argued that negative truthmakers (as I would now put it) can be dispensed with *entirely*. My argument required mention of *all* the positive properties of objects, but failed to discuss the problem of general truths that this raises.

Lewis puts great store by this principle. But there are upholders of Truthmaker Maximalism, such as C. B. Martin and George Molnar, who would be unmoved. Necessary connections between distinct existences? 'Yes', they will say. They think, for instance, that such connections can hold between cause and effect. And their position on causality is at least an arguable one.

My attachment to the Distinct Existences principle is somewhat less than it used to be. Let me try, nevertheless, to defend the truthmaker principle here while still trying to cleave to the principle for this case at least. The first two of the Lewis 'unicorn replacements' do stand under strong suspicion of flouting Distinct Existences. But, I think, the matter is much less clear in the case of a suitable general fact.

Consider the molecular fact or state of affairs that is the conjunction of all the lower-order facts or states of affairs. Assume that all these are positive. Now consider the further state of affairs, as Russell, and I after him, take it to be, that these *are* all the lower-order states of affairs. Notice, *contra* Lewis, that it does not involve states of affairs of everything being a non-unicorn. That everything is a non-unicorn seems to supervene, supervening harmlessly and without metaphysical cost, on the higher-order state of affairs. Rather, it is Plato's *difference*. Everything that exists is different from a unicorn.

This limit state of affairs, as we may call it, is of course not a mere mereological addition to the big molecular state of affairs. If it were such an add-on, then Lewis's stricture would have point. The big molecular state of affairs, the huge conjunction, is one of the *constituents* of the limit state of affairs. Just what the form of the limit state of affairs is, is a difficult matter (as Russell conceded), one that we still need to discuss later in this chapter. But it is clear that the limiter enfolds the big molecular state of affairs *in* a state of affairs. It can certainly be said that the big molecular state and the limiter are not identical. But although not identical, they are not *wholly* distinct. I think we should say that the big molecular state of affairs is a *non-mereological part* of the limiter.

Lewis, of course, does not think that there are such entities as facts or states of affairs. For him the only metaphysically respectable notion of a part is a mereological part. But perhaps he would have conceded this much: if, *per impossibile*, there were states of affairs, then the particulars, properties and relations that are their constituents would be non-mereological parts of the states of affairs.

The situation with the limiter is no different from the situation with more ordinary states of affairs. Suppose there is a state of affairs of *a*'s having F. This has as constituents *a* and F. These constituents are non-mereological parts of the state of affairs. The state of affairs is 'something more' than the mereological sum of its constituents, but it is not a further part, except in some *very* stretched sense.

6.2. THE LOGICAL FORM OF GENERAL FACTS

But how are we to analyse general facts? In the *Logical Atomism* lectures Russell says:

> I do not profess to know what the right analysis of general facts is. It is an exceedingly difficult question, and one I should very much like to see studied. (1972, p. 94)

In fact there has been little attention paid to the question. The general line of my argument has already been presented (in my 1989a, 7.2, and 1997, 13.2), but can hardly be omitted here. We will begin by confining ourselves to truths where a number of existents (which may be objects or states of affairs) are said to be *all* the existents of a certain sort. My idea is that the truthmakers for such truths are facts, states of affairs, having the following form: a relation, which I will here call the Tot relation, holds between a certain mereological object and a certain property ('T' being reserved for truthmakers). I am primarily, at least, concerned with contingent existents and contingent Tot relations.

'Tot' here stands, of course, for 'totality'. A certain mereological object *totals* a certain property. The mereological object is the whole composed of the existents in question. For myself, in agreement here with Lewis, I accept Unrestricted Mereological Composition of all existents whatsoever, however heterogeneous and/or numerous they may be. (I feel free to accept this principle because I think it involves no ontological cost, no addition of being. See Armstrong, 1997, p. 13.)

What about the property to which the mereological whole or manifold bears the Tot relation, the totalling relation? For innumerable cases the property will have to be, to use Lewis's terminology, an 'abundant' rather than a 'sparse' property. Suppose there are some black swans on the lake now. The mereological whole of these swans will total the (distinctly second-rate property) *black swan on the lake now*. That state of affairs (also second-rate), I am suggesting, is the truthmaker for the truth that this object is (these objects are) all the black swans on the lake now. (Notice that it is an *instantiated* property, instantiated at least once within the mereological object. So there are no worries about uninstantiated properties.) Here we have a dyadic relation holding between this object and this property. The object may be said to *all* this property, that is, set a limit to the instantiations of this property. There are no other black swans on the lake now.

Consider the aggregate, finite or infinite as it may be, of the electrons. The aggregate stands in a highly specific relation to the instantiated property (instantiated within that aggregate) of *being an electron*. That property may be said to *total* or to *all* that particular aggregate. The property has this totalling or alling relation to no other aggregate. Consider, again, the aggregate, finite or infinite as it may be, of the protons. The aggregate stands in a highly specific relation to the instantiated property (instantiated within that aggregate) of *being a proton*. The property has this totalling or alling relation to no other aggregate. These highly specific relations are, I suggest, the very same relation, apparently a universal. (Alternatively, they are exactly similar trope relations. It seems that my theory of the 'ontology of allness' could be accepted by a trope theorist with this – quite usual – substitution of exact similarity for identity.)

It can hardly be denied that such a relation exists (a point I failed to stress in earlier expositions). It looks to be exactly the same relation in each case, to be a true universal if you accept universals. This makes way for the hypothesis that states of affairs of aggregates having the form:

Tot (the aggregate, the corresponding property)

are the truthmakers, the ontological grounds, for truths of the form <this aggregate of Xs is all the Xs>. ('Aggregate' here is to be read as *mereological* aggregate. Unrestricted Mereological Composition is assumed.) It is not denied, of course, that the totalling or alling relation involves negation. It sets a limit to the things of that sort. Nor do I think we need worry about what must be admitted to be a thin, jejune notion of property, such as *swan on the lake now*, that is often involved. Where the aggregate is, the corresponding property has instances, and has them nowhere else. In any case, we may, I think, say that these instantiations of these second-rate properties supervene on, and are no ontological addition to, 'are nothing over and above' in the old and good phrase, the instantiation of the 'sparse', the 'true', properties and relations.

The form of these states of affairs is in each case Tot (a mereological whole, a property). The Tot relation is to be found even where there is just one object of a certain sort. There was said to be just one phoenix.

Supposing this to be so, we have Tot (a certain particular bird, *being a phoenix*). In fact, though, a negative existential is true: <there are no phoenixes>. The truthmaker for this latter proposition is then of a different form. See 6.1 and 6.2.1.

We are now in a position to say what are the truthmakers (or false-makers) for an ordinary general proposition such as 'All ravens are black'. (I deliberately avoid saying a universally quantified proposition, because the primary cases for truthmaking theory seem to be those where the subject term is both universally quantified *and has existential import*.) There are, *prima facie*, two totalities: the mereological whole of the black ravens and the mereological whole of the ravens. The truthmakers for these being the totalities that they are have already been indicated. (The first totals the property of *being a black raven*, the second totals the property of *being a raven*.) It then becomes clear that if and only if the two totalities are identical, then the proposition is true, and this one totality is its (minimal) truthmaker. If there are two distinct totalities, with the totality of the black ravens no more than a proper part of the totality of ravens, then the proposition is made false (as strictly it is in fact false, because of the rare existence of albino ravens).

It is understood, of course, that none of this is supposed to be any sort of definition or reductive explanation of the meaning of 'all', or the concept of *allness*. *Allness*, totality, I take to be a primitive conception which cannot be analysed away. All we can do is to try to chart its connection with other fundamental categories of being.

The centrally important case, though, is Russell's own case: the general fact that all the facts (states of affairs) of lower order *are* all such facts. The analysis in terms of the Tot relation is the same. The object is the mereological whole (or manifold) of all the lower-order states of affairs. The property involved in the relation is the very abstract one of *being a state of affairs*, a highest determinable above states of affairs. If the world is a world of states of affairs alone, as I contend, then we have another Tot relation holding between the very same whole and the 'property' *being any existent at all*. These states of affairs are the biggest states of affairs of all. Given these huge states of affairs, each positive, all the lesser totality or limit states of affairs are also given. In the great catalogue of being, as it were, you need neither have any of the lesser *allings* nor, I have claimed, any other negative states of affairs.

Before ending this section I will consider an objection put to me by one of the anonymous referees for this book. The referee asked whether there could be two possible worlds that differed in just one respect: one having and the other lacking the 'that's all' fact. This is clearly silly, which suggests that there is no totality fact or state of affairs that needs to be added to the world. In response, it is important to remember that totality facts are higher-order facts, with the lower-order entities that the totality facts 'collect' being a constituent of the totality fact. There are indefinite numbers of possible worlds where the lower-order entities all exist just as they do in the actual world, but do not constitute the totality of being. These are those possible worlds that have the actual world as a proper part. It is these worlds that constitute the proper contrast with the actual world. They give us worlds where the actual totality fact is missing. It may still be objected that the grand totality fact has the peculiarity that there *has* to be such a fact. Each of the possible worlds that contain the whole actual world must, after all, have their own grand totality fact. But even here, it would seem, there could be a world that lacked a totality fact. This would be the empty world. At 7.4 it will be argued, I admit somewhat tentatively, that the empty world is a possibility.

6.2.1. Minimal truthmakers for general and negative truths

It has just been argued that the biggest totality state of all, the one em-bracing all lower-order states of affairs, is all that we need to provide a truthmaker for all lesser totality truths – <these are all the black swans on this lake at present> – and all negative truths – <this swan is not white>. But, of course, when it comes to supplying *minimal* (or near-minimal) truthmakers, then lesser truthmakers suffice. The totality of this swan's properties, or even the totality of the properties of its plumage, will do for the swan not being white. (An Incompatibilist could argue that all that is required is the state of affairs of the swan's being black.)

We should at this point also take a look at negative existential truths: the non-existence of arctic penguins, the phoenix, unicorns, centaurs and the like that traditionally bedevil and enthral philosophers. It is quite often assumed – even in truthmaking circles – that the whole world is required as truthmakers for these truths.[2] This seems far too pessimistic. The (minimal) truthmaker for <there are no arctic penguins> would seem to be the arctic animals (including whatever is the truthmaker for their being animals and

---

[2] This assumption perhaps derives from the assumption that <there are no unicorns> ought to be put in the form <for all *x*, *x* is not a unicorn>. Then the whole world, all the *x*s, might seem to be required.

living in the arctic), together with the state of affairs that these are the totality of such animals. Each of the arctic animals is, by its nature, *different* from a penguin, as Plato might have said, so this general state of affairs seems truthmaker enough for this negative existential. In the same way, if we work with the totality of all birds, we eliminate the phoenix.

In the case of unicorns we need first the horse-like creatures plus the usual totality state of affairs that collects all such animals. It must further be true of each of these creatures that they lack unicorn-making characteristics (uni-hornedness, etc.), and so there must be totality states of affairs involving each one of the horse-like creatures to act as truthmakers for these lacks. In the case of centaurs we can begin with the collection of horse-bodies, and then proceed in much the same way. It is, no doubt, a somewhat imprecise matter what is to count as a horse-like object – could there be horses on a planet elsewhere in space-time? – but we can bracket all such problems. The minimal truthmakers will have to be fairly extensive, as all truthmakers involving totality and negativity tend to be. But the point I have been concerned to make in this section is that the minimal truthmakers need not embrace the whole world.

6.3. TOTALITY STATES OF AFFAIRS AND THE CAUSAL ORDER

A difficulty that may be (indeed, should be) proposed is that totality states of affairs fail the Eleatic Stranger's plausible demand (*Sophist*, 247e) that it is a mark of the real that it should bestow power. That all things of a certain sort are indeed *all* of that sort does not seem to be a power-bestowing factor in the way the world proceeds.

But we can, I hope, somewhat weaken the Eleatic Principle without losing plausibility. Let us demand only that every truthmaker should make *some* contribution to the causal order of the actual world. It should play *some causal role*. This does not, alas, seem to be a necessary truth, but it is hard to see how we could ever have any good reason to postulate things that play no causal role at all. A question therefore arises what is the causal role of totality states of affairs.

I think we can avail ourselves here of C. B. Martin's distinction between the causally operative and the causally relevant. Totality states of affairs, it must be conceded, are not causally operative. But they are, in general at least, causally relevant. The relevance can be spelt out in terms of causal counterfactuals, Dowe counterfactuals in particular (see 5.2.2 for these sort of counterfactuals). The totality of mammals in this room at the present time of writing is two. This-room-now *twos* the property of being a mammal. Absent a miracle, mammalian additions to the room now would require a difference in the past and the future of the whole world. The same holds for the subtraction of one or both of the mammals. This, we may suggest, is the causal relevance of this particular totality state of affairs.

But counterfactuals, of course, like any other truth, require truthmakers. What will the truthmakers be for the whole raft of true counterfactuals involving in their antecedent the presence of various collections of extra mammals in the room now? It seems that a very large truthmaker indeed will be required, appropriately enough, perhaps, for a totality state of affairs. At least the room itself at that time will be needed, together with large swathes of its spatiotemporal environment. The relevant laws of nature will be needed, or if the 'laws of nature' are taken to be truths only, then whatever are the proper truthmakers for these truths. With different mammals and different numbers of mammals in the antecedents of the different counterfactuals, truthmakers for truths about the nature and behaviour of the mammals in question will also be required. There is reason to think that counterfactual truths are a sort of second-rate discourse, metaphysically speaking, and that their truthmakers cannot be identified with great precision. But the way the world actually is and the way it actually works (in particular in respect to this room and in respect to mammals) seems to serve to make such truths true, where they are true. And this, I suggest, constitutes the causal relevance of states of affairs of totality. Things would have been caused to be different if the state of totality had not obtained.

Suppose, again, that the great world-embracing totality state of affairs that actually obtains had not obtained. The world would have been bigger or smaller. If smaller, then this would presumably have made a difference, if only here and there, to the way the remainder of reality behaved. If larger, presumably that would have made a difference also. It is true that it would not have made a difference if the extra entities were epiphenomenal, but that possibility is itself inconsistent with the Eleatic Principle. Again, it would have made no difference *here* if the extra entities were, say, in a space-time causally cut off from our space-time. Even so, there would have been different causal activity in that other realm. The causal relevance for the smaller totality states of affairs within the all-inclusive state of affairs seems even more obvious. So it seems that totality states are causally relevant via counterfactuals. As indicated earlier, the truthmakers for the counterfactuals will be the relevant laws of nature, taken ontologically, and the relevant boundary conditions.

6.3.1. Cox's objection

There is still, however, a particular difficulty that faces the notion of a highest-order state of affairs that embraces all the states of affairs below it. Will this not produce a paradoxical, or semi-paradoxical, situation similar to Cantor's paradox about the class of all classes? The difficulty has been urged by Damian Cox in 'The trouble with truth-makers' (1997). I anticipated, and tried to meet, the difficulty that Cox raises in my *A World of States of Affairs* (1997, pp. 198–9), an anticipation that I believe constitutes an answer. So I will go over the same general line of thought here.

The highest-order state of affairs bundles together all lower-order states of affairs. But, the argument runs, the real *totality* of states of affairs is these lower-order states plus the highest-order state. Will not a still higher-order state of affairs be required to collect all states of affairs, including the great collector? An infinite regress is off and running. At the very best, it may be urged, there is a colossal failure of economy.

The argument, however, depends on the fact that, because the first collector is itself a state of affairs, though of higher order, a further collector will be required, and so forever. My idea is to answer the difficulty by *conceding* that here we really do have a regress of *truths*. But we know from the general theory of truthmaking that different truths can all have the same truthmaker. So I suggest that what we have here, after the first collector, is no more than a series of truths which all have the very same truthmaking state of affairs, viz. the original 'Russellian' totality state of affairs. The necessity at each step after the first at least suggests that no increase of being is involved. I cannot *prove* that this is so. 'Suggests' is not proof. The postulation of schemes of truthmakers is, as has been emphasized in this work, not susceptible of strict proof. But it looks quite plausible. The difficulty that we have just been considering always looked like a bit of philosopher's thought-play.

There is a parallel, though admittedly in a simpler case. Suppose $<p>$ is true, then $<p$ is true$>$ is true, $<$it is true that p is true$>$ is true, and so forever. Do we think that each of these truths (in some sense, different truths) each requires its own distinct truthmaker? A metaphysician without worries about economy could argue for such a requirement. And I do not see how to *refute* the view. But a more natural position seems to be that all these truths have the very same truthmakers, the truthmakers for $<p>$. Our symbolisms permit the regress, but it does not have ontological significance. No increase of being is involved. May we not put forward the same hypothesis in the case of the regress of totality states of affairs? Another regress would be: with $<p>$ true, $<\neg\neg p$ is true$>$, $<\neg\neg\neg\neg p$ is true$>$, and so on. Again, different truths, same truthmaker.

In the case of the truth regress it may be suggested, not implausibly, that all we have is a regress of sentences.[3] And then some may wish to extend this point to cover the apparent regress of states of affairs. I think that this is a minor matter. If there is a 'realm of propositions', some true and some false, then presumably it must definitely include or exclude such steps in the regresses under consideration. But the *naturalist* will want to say that the line between propositions, statements and even sentences is somewhat fluid and vague at the borders of these classes of entities. We should, I think, firmly link propositions with being true or not being true. But having said that, what is to count as a proposition, and whether in a particular case we have just one or two propositions, in cases of the sort that we are discussing, may be an essentially imprecise matter. Another case worth thinking about here is contraposition. $<$All A are B$>$ is logically equivalent to $<$All non-B are non-A$>$. Do we have two different true propositions, or one proposition but two statements, or even one proposition but two sentences? I incline to say two truths, but I recognize that there may be some stipulation here.

6.4. WHY DID RUSSELL WANT BOTH GENERAL FACTS AND NEGATIVE FACTS?

Russell, however, saw the need both for general facts *and* negative facts. Why? One might have thought that his avowed commitment to Occam's razor would have led him away from this relatively uneconomical scheme.

A clue may perhaps be found in *The Philosophy of Logical Atomism*, where he says:

We have such propositions as 'All men are mortal' and 'Some men are Greeks'. But you have not only such *propositions*; you have also such *facts*, and that, of course, is where you get back to the inventory of the world: that, in addition to particular facts, . . . there are also general facts and existence-facts, that is to say, there are not merely *propositions* of that sort but also *facts* of that sort. (1972, pp. 91–2)

---

[3] See Hochberg's discussion of a Bradley regress on p. 169 of his 1999. There he says, 'Facts [my states of affairs] are recognized as truth makers, but the original fact can be taken to suffice as the truth ground for the series of ensuing sentences of increasing complexity.' This seems to be essentially the same move as the one I have just made in meeting Cox's argument. The distinction between sentences and truths seems not too important in this context.

Here Russell is countenancing 'existence-facts' as well as particular facts. Yet it would seem that all he really needed was particular facts by themselves, because, as already argued, they will necessitate all the existence-facts.

It seems to me that Russell must be rejecting, consciously or unconsciously, what I have suggested is a plausible general principle in truthmaker theory. The principle is the Entailment principle that if a truthmaker T necessitates truth *t*, and *t* entails *u*, then in general, even if not in special cases, T will also be a truthmaker for *u*. Russell must be thinking that *u* will have a different truthmaker from *t*. If, however, one accepts the Entailment principle in this context, then one can maintain that particular facts (states of affairs) and general facts (states of affairs) suffice as truthmakers for negative truths and existential truths.

6.5. NEW THINKING ABOUT GENERAL FACTS

At 4.4 I drew attention to Donald Baxter's idea that the link between universals and the particulars that instantiate them should be taken to be one of 'intersection' or partial identity. Such a partial identity, Baxter urges, would provide a solution to the traditional difficulty, first discussed by Plato in his dialogue the *Parmenides*, of how universals stand to their particulars. Among those who accept universals in contemporary philosophy it is customary to hold that the way that they stand to particulars is a *contingent* matter (although exception is often made for essential properties of particulars). Baxter continues to accept this contingency (Baxter, 2001). I find the partial identity very attractive, but it seems to me that partial identity, like any identity, brings necessity with it. If a universal is partially identical with a certain particular, then to try to consider that very universal without it being instantiated by that particular is to consider a mere counterpart of the universal in question.

Suppose that this is correct. Let us consider in the light of this what are the truthmakers for the truth <these particulars, *a, b, c*, ... are all the Fs> where F is a universal. Each of the predications <*a* is F>, <*b* is F>, ... will be necessary in virtue of the partial identities involved. If we consider the possibility of any of these particulars not being F, then we should say that strictly speaking this is not a possibility. It could only be a counterpart of F that lacked any of its instances. Again, if we consider the possibility of a particular being F although in fact it does not instantiate F, then again we are considering a mere counterpart of F. The property F must have all its instances and it cannot have any others. But if this is so, the conjunction of states of affairs *a's being F & b's being F* ... will serve as truthmaker for the truth <this conjunction is all the Fs>. *Allness* will supervene in this situation. A Russellian general fact or state of affairs will not be needed in addition. General facts seemed needed only because <this conjunction is all the Fs> was taken to be contingent.

A still more spectacular vision seems to open. Given all the particulars and all the first-order universals, then all the states of affairs are fixed. They are fixed because states of affairs, on this view, are intersections, partial identities, of the particulars and universals. And for anyone who thinks that the world may be assayed as a world of states of affairs, the nature of the world is fixed. Compare the situation with *non-transferable* tropes. Given that a trope (property or relation) must attach to the particular it does attach to (or must belong to the bundle it belongs to), then all states of affairs are fixed.

There remains a place for contingency in this scheme. The particulars and the universals, or the particulars and the tropes, are contingent beings. Given that they are what they are, they link up in a certain way necessarily. But they themselves are contingent. There might have been different particulars and universals, or different particulars and tropes, and then there would have been different states of affairs. The necessary connection we have here is a necessary connection between contingent entities.

Notice that even if this line of thought is correct, there seems to be need for at least one totality state of affairs. For even if it is *extensionally* correct to say, for instance, that reality is exhausted by states of affairs having particulars and universals as their constituents, it seems not to be a necessary truth that this is so. If this is correct, then the further truth that <and this is all> will require a further truthmaker, a totality state of affairs as I have argued.

6.6. *IN MEMORIAM*: GEORGE MOLNAR

In his fine article already mentioned (Molnar, 2000) George Molnar argued that there are four extremely plausible theses, which, however, cannot all be true:

(i) The world is everything that exists
(ii) Everything that exists is positive
(iii) Some negative claims about the world are true

(iv) Every true claim about the world is made true by something that exists.

Molnar left the problem there. He had no solution. I submit with respect that in this situation the least evil is to reject (ii). The postulation of totality states of affairs, or at least one such state of affairs, is my way of doing that. Limits, if not absences, are ontological realities.

7

Truthmakers for modal truths,
part 1: possibility

7.1. INTRODUCTION

The question of truthmakers for modal truths is in considerable disarray. Many philosophers who are sympathetic to the idea of truthmakers are nevertheless influenced by the *Tractatus* picture, where contingent truths are made true by the atomic facts (with some apparent uncertainty about contingent negative and contingent general truths), but modal truths, in particular necessary truths, lack truthmakers because they 'all say the same thing, viz. nothing'.

7.2. THE POSSIBILITY PRINCIPLE

We are concerned with the weakest grade of possibility: metaphysical possibility. Necessities are possibilities. If p is necessary, then p is possible. Contingent truths are also possibilities. (A contingent proposition is one where both the proposition and its contradictory, p & $\neg p$, are possible.) If p is contingently true, then p is possible. But the philosophically interesting possibilities are the contingent falsities. Call these propositions the 'mere possibilities'. These yield a body of modal truths: truths having the form 'it is possible that p' where, however, p itself is false ($\neg p$ & $\diamond p$). What truthmakers shall we propose for these 'truths of mere possibility'?

It seems to me very surprising that so many good philosophers consider that huge metaphysical commitments must be made in order to give an account of these truths. David Lewis (1986) postulated a whole pluriverse: 'the worlds in all their glory'. Alvin Plantinga (1974) rejects these other worlds, but adds to this world, our world, an uncountable multitude of sets of propositions, each set a way that the world might have been, but is in fact not. (Roughly, for each one of Lewis's worlds Plantinga has such a set.) My thesis is that these philosophers are bringing in giants to do a boy's work. 'Possible worlds' are useful fictions, no doubt, but we ought to be looking for quite modest truthmakers, fairly deflationary truthmakers, for these fairly unimportant truths of mere possibility.

Consider any contingent truth, p. Since it is true, it follows that not-p is false. <It is possible that not-p> is nevertheless true. For each contingent truth, a shadow truth accompanies it: the possibility (metaphysical possibility) of its contradictory. It is a 'mere' possibility only. Given p, and given that it is contingent, the truth <it is possible that not-p> is entailed.

This entailment should make us wonder. May we not validly use the Entailment principle in this context? (Apparently even if the entailment is classical.) Consider one of p's truthmakers, T. May it not be a truthmaker (not necessarily a *minimal* truthmaker) for <it is possible that not-p>? We cannot appeal here to the amended Jackson thesis (2.5), because that only says that where a 'purely' contingent truth entails a purely contingent truth, then any truthmaker for the entailing proposition is a truthmaker for the entailed proposition. Most philosophers, including myself, would take <it is possible that not-p> to be a necessary truth, so it would not fall under the Jackson thesis. But although a necessary truth, it is very tightly linked to the truth T. It is at least plausible to say that the connection is analytic, that it holds in virtue of what we mean by the phrase 'contingent proposition'. At least, surely, we can say this: it is of the essence of contingency that the contradictory of a contingent truth be a possibility. Under these conditions, it seems reasonable to say that a truthmaker for a contingent truth is *also* a truthmaker for the truth that the contradictory of that truth is possible. At a stroke, we have removed the need for any truthmakers for truths of 'mere possibility' except the truthmakers for contingent truths.

Here is the argument spelt out more formally:

1. (T $\rightarrow$ p) (assumed)
2. <p is contingent> (assumed)
3. p entails <it is possible that not-p> (from 2 and the nature of the contingency of propositions)
4. $\therefore$ T $\rightarrow$ <it is possible that not-p> (by 1, 3 and the Entailment principle)[1]

We remember that the connective '$\rightarrow$' is not an entailment, but a cross-categorial necessity. T is something in the world, some state of affairs or other entity depending on exactly what truthmakers are postulated, a matter that depends on one's whole metaphysics. Given the attractive

---

[1] I am grateful to Marian David for pointing out a simplification of my argument here.

S5 modal system, if p is contingent, it is a necessary truth that it is contingent. This may help to quell any doubts one may have about step 3 in the argument. We may also notice how attractive it is to hold that *every* contingent truth, not merely every *positive* contingent truth, has a truthmaker. Given this, the Entailment principle can then give the attractive result, attractive for those looking for system and coherence, that these simple *but relevant* truthmakers exist for *every* 'mere possibility'. I dub this the Possibility principle.

The need for far-fetched truthmakers such as really existing possible worlds seems removed. Someone might still wish to postulate as truthmakers for mere possibilities a realm or realms of possibilities in ontological addition to actualities. As usual, nothing in my argument rules this out. But the pressure to make this ontological addition seems much reduced. Occamist considerations become very weighty. Notice again that one is not committed to the idea that the truthmaker for a contingent truth, even if it is a minimal truthmaker for that truth, is necessarily a *minimal* truth for the associated possibility that it is false. Minimal truthmakers for truths of possibility are discussed at 7.5.

There is a still simpler argument that seems to have weight. We can first give a nominal definition of 'contingent being': an entity C is a contingent being if and only if 'C exists' is a contingent truth. The predicate 'might not have existed' is true of such a C. Consider now the totality of contingent beings. If any of these beings were not to exist, and/or any further contingent beings were to exist, then the 'mere possibilities' would have to vary with these differences. That is to say, the mere possibilities supervene upon the actual contingent beings. Any difference in the realm of the contingent would involve a difference in the mere possibilities. This consideration, of course, does not show us in any detail what are the truthmakers for the truths of mere possibility. (This is a general limitation of supervenience theses for truthmaker theory.) But it casts some further cold water on the need for the wildly ambitious truthmakers that have been proposed by a number of contemporary metaphysicians.

For this second argument, there is in any case the question as to what metaphysical interpretation we should place on this supervenience. I wish to interpret it as showing that the mere possibilities are no addition of being to the contingent beings that they supervene upon. Compare the necessary supervenience of the mental on the physical. This is a controversial doctrine, of course, but one that is normally taken to imply that the mental is no addition of being to the physical. 'No addition of being' does not mean that the mental does not exist. It is not a charter for elim-inativism. In the same way, the supervenience of the mere possibilities does not mean that it is untrue that there are such possibilities. But it does mean, I contend, that these possibilities are not something ontologically *additional* to the contingent existences.

If the Possibility principle gives us satisfactory truthmakers for the mere possibilities, then the other possibilities should be easy enough. If *p* is *true* and contingent, then surely the truthmakers for *p* should be truthmakers for the possibility of *p*. (Of course, a minimal truthmaker for *p* will not normally be a *minimal* truthmaker for the possibility of *p*.) If *p* is neces-sary, then whatever truthmakers we find for necessary truths should be truthmakers (again perhaps not minimal) for the possibility of *p*.

A matter that may be thought to require attention is the matter of the *extension* of the realm of contingency. It is important to notice that nothing in the argument of this section casts any light on this matter. For some the laws of nature (I am taking the phrase 'laws of nature' ontologically) are contingent, but for others they are necessary. For most analytic philoso-phers, an attribution of a property to a particular is contingent. But we have seen in 4.4–5 that this can be denied both by trope theorists and up-holders of universals. The particular and the property may be contingent beings – I think they are – but *the particular's having the property* may be a necessity. At the same time I still favour the hypothesis that particulars, properties, states of affairs and laws of nature are all of them contingent beings. Their links, or some of their links, to each other may be necessary but they, I hypothesize, are all contingent beings. (It is this that allows the possibility of the empty world. See 7.4.)

7.3. THE POSSIBILITY OF ALIENS

An apparent possibility that now requires discussion is the possibility of what David Lewis named 'aliens'; alien particulars, properties and relations. These entities are *non-actual* particulars or properties or relations which, furthermore and very importantly, are not 'combinatorially constructible' from actual particulars, properties and relations. I take it that 'combina-torially constructible' is readily intelligible at the intuitive level at least. There are no unicorns, but unicorns are combinatorially constructible from things that do exist: horses, horns and so on.

For Lewis there are non-actual things that exist. They are to be found in other possible worlds from our world, but they are none the less existents, he maintains. Since on his view particulars cannot be identical across worlds, although they have 'counterparts' in other worlds, all other-worldly particulars must be aliens relative to our world. But are there alien properties and relations in some of his other worlds? It cannot, he says, be proved that there are, but it is immensely plausible, given his premises, to suppose that there are. Why should the properties and relations instantiated in other worlds all be either the same as those instantiated in ours, or be constructible from the ones instantiated in ours? Some worlds may be rich in properties and relations that are not constructible from the properties and relations of our own world.

If instead there is, as I hold, of necessity only one world, the case is altered. Alien particulars cannot exist, by definition. They belong, at best, with the *merely* possible. A metaphysician might still construct a sort of surrogate for aliens by allowing *uninstantiated* properties and relations: these might be said to be *relative* aliens, alien relative to the *instantiated* properties or relations.[2] (That is to say: other than the instantiated properties and relations and not constructible from them.) But if uninstantiated properties and relations are denied, as I myself hold that they should be denied, then even this way of providing truthmakers for aliens is blocked. The possibility that they should exist is the possibility that they should be instantiated, and that is, at best, a *mere* possibility.

Notice that the issue is not epistemological. Suppose we believe that we have a good catalogue (given to us by physics, perhaps) of the fundamental properties and relations that are instantiated. We may still wonder whether we are perhaps mistaken and instead that there exist further properties and relations not combinatorially accessible from the ones catalogued. Perhaps, we may surmise, these further properties and relations are epistemically inaccessible to us. Suppose that there are such properties. We could call them epistemic aliens. But they would not be ontological aliens, and it is the ontological aliens that we are concerned with here.

The problem that the ontological aliens pose is this. Although by defini-tion aliens do not exist, can we not say with truth that aliens are possible? There might have been further particulars in the world, and ones not combinatorially constructible from the actual particulars. A duck in this room now, a room at present without any ducks, but a duck not composed of any of the particulars that compose the actual world, would be such a

---

[2] Perhaps there could exist ghostly particulars also, such as Father Christmas, having some sort of 'abstract' being. But I shall ignore this unappetizing option.

case. Again, there might have been further properties and relations in the world, and ones not combinatorially constructible from the actual properties and relations. We can hardly give examples in this case (although I have sometimes been asked for them!) but this modal statement has the ring of truth. But if it is true, what is its truthmaker? What truthmakers can a one-worlder offer for the proposition <alien properties and particulars are possible>?

In the past I was at first so daunted by the problem of finding truthmakers for these statements that I suggested that alien properties and relations, in particular, are not in fact metaphysical possibilities at all. They are, I argued in *A Combinatorial Theory of Possibility* (1989a, 4.1), merely conceptual possibilities, perhaps like the 'possibility' that water is *not* composed of H_2O. If Kripke is right, although this is thinkable, is conceivable, it is nevertheless impossible. In *A World of States of Affairs* (1997, 10.4), I took this conceptualist account of the aliens back and granted that the existence of alien properties and relations is a genuine possibility, although, of course, a mere possibility. But my attempt to find truthmakers for these truths of possibility was not very satisfactory, and I expressed doubt about it at the time.

I start now from the position that alien particulars, properties and relations are possible. No aliens can exist, they are *merely* possible, but they are possible. Their possibility seems to be denied by Wittgenstein in the *Tractatus*, and was in the past denied by me, but this position seems implausible. What truthmakers can I offer? My present suggestion rests on two premises. First there is the Possibility principle already argued for in 7.2 that, given a contingent truth, its truthmakers, whatever they may be, will also be truthmakers for the modal truth that the contradictory of the contingent truth is (metaphysically) possible. (By Truthmaker Maximalism the truth will have a truthmaker.) Second there is Russell's insight that contingent general truths, that is, contingent universally quantified truths, require *general facts*, or, as I like to put it, totality states of affairs, as their truthmaker.

Assuming, as we have agreed, that aliens are genuine metaphysical possibilities, then, since they are by definition *mere* possibilities (for one-worlders), the biggest fact (state of affairs) of all will be a truthmaker for these possibilities. But fairly obviously it is not a *minimal* truthmaker. To find minimal truthmakers, we must still appeal to general facts, totality states of affairs, but they will be more limited ones. So let us work for simplicity with properties alone, and further let us make the assumption – again for the purpose of simplifying – that all structural properties, all complex properties, are composed of *simple* properties and relations. This, as I take it, is one of the assumptions of logical atomism, and it may be true (epistemic 'may' only).

Given this assumption, consider the totality of all the simple properties. Are they the only *possible* simple properties? As already argued, it seems incorrect to say so. It is a contingent truth, I would argue, that each simple property exists. They are contingent beings. A further contingent truth is <these simple properties are the totality of the simple properties>. This truth has a truthmaker (a totality fact, according to me). The following is a modal truth: <there might have been further simple properties than these>. So we have the premises needed to apply the Possibility principle. By that principle the truthmaker for the modal truth is the truthmaker for the non-modal truth <these simple properties are the totality of the simple properties>.

The truthmaker for this truth is a contingent general fact, a totality state of affairs: that a certain collection of simple properties is *all* the simple properties that there are. (In my own suggested analysis of this sort of state of affairs given in chapter 6: a certain collection of simple properties *totals* the 'property' of *being a simple property*.) And since it is a contingent fact or state of affairs, by the argument of the previous section it will be a truthmaker for the truth that <it is possible that it is *not* the case that this collection of simple properties is the totality of simple properties>. There might have been more. The actually existing simple properties are the truthmaker for the modal truth that there might have been more of them. And notice that the suggested truthmaker is a *minimal* truthmaker, and indeed is a *unique* minimal truthmaker.

Perhaps this example will suffice for the matter of the aliens. The principles involved in finding minimal truthmakers for other true modal claims about aliens should be clear enough. Notice particularly that general facts (states of affairs) are required to give this account of the aliens. The fact that the solution is so neat and simple seems to be a recommendation for those unpopular entities, Russellian general facts.

7.4. IS IT POSSIBLE FOR THERE TO BE NOTHING AT ALL?

If our account of 'mere possibilities' has been correct, then some light may be shed on the philosopher's question – who else could give it much scrutiny? – 'Could there have been nothing at all?'

Prima facie, the metaphysician can consider three options: (i) the world may contain nothing but one or more necessary beings – the Absolute and Spinoza's one substance are candidates; (ii) the world may contain both necessary beings and contingent beings – say, God and the numbers on the one hand, the space-time world on the other; (iii) the world is a world of contingent beings – the space-time world is the natural example. It is plausible that it does not contain any necessary beings. If either (i) or (ii) is correct, then the empty world is not a possibility. Necessary beings, after all, have to exist, so there has to be something. So let us grant (iii) for the purposes of this discussion; I incline towards it in any case.

Of course, if a necessary being is possible, then it exists. So if there are no necessary beings, it is impossible for there to be any. It is *necessary* that whatever exists is contingent. (Notice, however, that this would not by itself rule out necessary *connections* between the contingent existences. That there are no necessary connections between (wholly) distinct existences is a further interesting and controversial contention, a contention we associate with Hume.)

It is clear that <something exists> is true (*pace* Gorgias), and if that something is no more than a contingent being or beings (as we are assuming), then we can raise the question whether it is true that <it is possible that there could have been nothing>. If that is a possibility, it is a mere possibility only, but perhaps this modal proposition is true all the same. What would be its truthmaker? It seems that the formula given in 7.2 for finding truthmakers for mere possibilities, the Possibility principle, can be applied even to this arcane possibility.

Given the assumption that the world is a world of contingent beings, then <there is at least one contingent being> is a true proposition, one having innumerable truthmakers each of them sufficient by itself for the truth of this proposition. (Simple entities, if such exist, would perhaps be the only *minimal* truthmakers for this truth.) Now, provided that <there is at least one contingent being> is a *contingent* truth, the usual formula tells us that any truthmaker for this truth will also be the truthmaker for the modal proposition <there might have been no contingent being>. But in a world of contingent beings this is <the possibility of there being nothing at all>. We have the wanted truthmaker.

But is <there is at least one contingent being> really a contingent truth? It might be maintained that it is a necessary truth. It must obviously be conceded that for each contingent being, it might not have existed. But it may be suggested that it does not follow, and is not true, that the *totality* of contingent beings could not have existed. I do not find very attractive this idea that one can, as it were, subtract anything from the world yet it is nevertheless impossible to subtract everything. (See, in particular, the arguments advanced against it by Rodriguez-Pereyra, 1997.) There is, however, a consideration from truthmaking theory, pointed out to me by Bruin Christensen. Given a total absence of beings, he suggested there would be 'in that world' no truthmaker for the truth <there is nothing at all>. This made me wonder whether the empty world is really a possibility. On further consideration, however, I think this argument is to be rejected. It may have value in certain cases to consider what would be the truthmakers 'in another world'. The real truthmakers, though, are in this world. In this world, it would seem, we have truthmakers for <at least one contingent being exists>, and this truth is at least plausibly a contingent truth. The argument of 7.2 is that a truthmaker for a contingent truth is also truthmaker for the modal truth that it is possible that that contingent truth is not true. So why should we not maintain as a modal truth <it is possible that there might *not* have been any contingent being>? This, together with the rejection of necessary beings (something still to be argued for in the next chapter), gives us the possibility of the empty world.

7.5. MINIMAL TRUTHMAKERS FOR TRUTHS OF POSSIBILITY

It was argued at 7.2 that truths of mere possibility (*p* possible but not true) could be given a somewhat deflationary, but nevertheless relevant, truthmaker. This truthmaker is a truthmaker for the true <not-*p*>. (By Truthmaker Maximalism, <not-*p*> will always have a truthmaker.) It was pointed out, though, that very often the minimal truthmaker for <not-*p*> would not be a minimal truthmaker for the truth that <*p* is possible>. In this final section of this chapter we ask what are the *minimal* truthmakers for truths of possibility. This is not only of interest in itself, but will assist us in our next enquiry, the finding of truthmakers for truths of necessity.

It is convenient to begin by distinguishing between modal truths of the sort <it is possible that Xs exist> and those of the sort <it is possible that *a* is F>, although the solution of the two problems is not very different. Let us begin with possibilities of existence.

Consider, in particular, the cases where the entities in question do not exist, where they are *mere* possibilities. It is, let us suppose, true that <it is possible that a unicorn exists>. What then would be a minimal truthmaker for this truth? The obvious solution is combinatorial. The non-existent entity is some non-existent (but possible) combination out of elements that do exist. The phrase 'non-existent combination' may raise eyebrows. Am I committing myself to a Meinongian view? No, I say. The *elements* of the combination are, I assert, the only truthmakers that are needed for the truth that this combination is possible. Notice that combination may include indefinite repetition (even infinite repetition) of the sort of elements that allow of repetition. And since the non-existent can be no better than a merely *intentional* object, an object of thought, it may be a vague or indeterminate object, introducing a corresponding indeterminacy into just what elements are to be 'combined'. (This is on the assumption, which I incline to, that there is no vagueness in reality).

We do need it to be true that the elements are *combinable*, but this is all that we need. In this way, I hope, we can get past the great Meinong. What of the modal truth <these elements are combinable>? Here I suggest that the truthmaker for this truth is again no more than the elements themselves. Combinability is a relation, but it is surely an internal relation, because given the elements, their combinability or non-combinability is necessitated by their nature. And the truthmakers for internal relations, I have argued, are just the terms of the relation.

Some elements, of course, are not combinable. Roundness and squareness will not combine in the same object. These elements, *from their own nature*, are not combinable in this way. (These two elements are the truthmakers for <it is impossible that there be a round square>. See 8.8.) But the elements that go to make up the philosophers' menagerie, unicorns and so forth, are, I am assuming, combinable. It does not matter much if I am wrong in this assumption. The possibility (mere, of course) or impossibility of these imaginary animals is not very important for ontology!

Is there a general criterion, though, that one can give to mark off the combinable from the uncombinable? My suggestion is to appeal to the *form* of states of affairs or facts. This should provide at least a necessary condition. The simplest state of affairs is the first-order monadic one. It is exhausted by the following description: a property instantiated by a particular. That is its form. Two elements, then, with one a property and the other a particular, *prima facie* are minimal truthmakers for the modal truth <it is possible that this property is instantiated by this particular>. The treatment just given can then be extended to whatever sorts of states of affairs or facts that it proves necessary to postulate in our metaphysics. One advantage of this suggestion is that it does justice to the idea that properties and particulars are unsaturated entities that stand in need of each other to exist. I think that this is a plausible necessary condition. It would be nice if it were a sufficient condition also: that would give a free run to a combinatorialist account of possibility. That is a big further step that cannot be argued here. But even if I have given no more than a necessary condition, and further conditions are needed to give sufficiency, I would still argue that it is the elements all by themselves that provide minimal truthmakers or falsemakers for the modal propositions involved.

Turning to a different matter, what about things that really exist, such as horses and human beings? It is a truth that <human beings are possible objects>. Any human being will be a truthmaker for this truth. But here we are looking for *minimal* truthmakers for this truth, and the possibility of human beings does not depend on their existing. It seems that to get a minimal truthmaker we will again have to get down to ultimate, simple existents: simple particulars, properties and relations. Whatever simple objects it takes to make a human being – and there would be a great deal of semantic vagueness here, of course – will be the minimal truthmakers for this possibility. Once again, we do not seem to need the *states of affairs* in which these simple particulars would have, as I'd argue, to be organized to get a human being. The *possibility* of such states of affairs would be enough, and for that possibility the simple objects would be the truthmakers. (This, by the way, seems to be at least in the spirit of the *Tractatus*.)

We may notice, though, that if there are truly simple entities, then the truth <simple entity S exists> and the truth <it is possible that simple entity S exists> both have exactly the same minimal (and unique) truthmaker. This truthmaker is the simple object itself. (Query: but does simplicity demand a totality condition in addition?)

The solutions that have just been suggested have to meet an obvious objection, though. What if there are no genuine atoms? What if every particular, property and relation is a structure, so that there are 'structures all the way down'? This may or may not be a metaphysical possibility, but it is surely an epistemic possibility. From this difficulty, however, we are released by Greg Restall's notable insight (2.12) that where certain truths involving infinity are involved (if there are such truths, i.e. provided that there really is infinity in the world), minimal truthmakers can be lacking. (To remind: given a denumerable number of, say, electrons, then there can be no minimal truthmaker for the truth that there is a denumerable number of electrons.) If an existent structure goes 'all the way down', is infinite in extent, then there *is* no minimal truthmaker for the truth that such a structure is possible. Some truthmakers will be *more minimal* relative to other truthmakers for the same truth, but that is the best we can say.

We can now turn to the question of minimal truthmakers for truths of the form <it is possible that a is F>. The answer is much the same as truths of the form <it is possible that an X exists>. Assuming that a and F both exist, the answer will be: the mereological sum of whatever is the minimal truthmaker for <a exists> plus whatever is the minimal truthmaker for <F exists>. If a and F are simples, then their sum is the minimal truthmaker required. If they are not simples, but their complexity is not an infinite complexity, then the mere mereological sum of their ultimate constituents will be the minimal truthmakers. If either a or F is infinitely complex, then minimal truthmakers for the modal truth cannot be had. If either a does not exist or the property F is not instantiated, then the elements of the combinatorial construction that yields a or F will be the minimal truthmakers.

8

Truthmakers for modal truths, part 2: necessity

So much for truthmakers for truths of possibility. Our task now is to tackle the more difficult problem of necessary truths.

8.1. AGAINST EXTENSIONAL ACCOUNTS OF NECESSITY

We will begin, however, by criticizing extensional accounts of necessity. Let us temporarily assume modal realism, the real existence of the Lewisian pluriverse which contains all possible worlds. If one tries to combine this assumption with the acceptance of truthmaker theory, then presumably one must say that necessary truths are those that have truthmakers in every world. For certain necessary truths we might wish to limit the worlds to ones that contain the entities that are involved in this truth. Thus, for the truth that $7 + 5 = 12$, we might restrict the worlds to those that contain at least twelve entities because smaller worlds, if there are such possible worlds, seem to furnish no truthmakers for this truth. But this restriction seems not particularly important here.

We pose once again that wonderful dilemma: the Euthyphro question. In the dialogue of that name, Socrates asks whether the piety of certain actions is constituted by the fact that the gods love these actions, or whether instead the acts are independently pious and *therefore* are loved by the gods. In the same sort of way, we can ask whether the necessity of a particular necessary truth is constituted by the fact that it has a truthmaker in all possible worlds, or whether instead the truth is independently necessary and *therefore* it has a truthmaker in all these worlds.

This particular specimen of a Euthyphro dilemma poses a choice between an *extensional* and an *intensional* account of necessary truth. ('Intensional' here does not take a semantic sense, of course.) And once the dilemma is posed, it seems natural and plausible to say that it is the fact that the necessary truth is *itself* necessary that determines its truth in all worlds. This intension determines its extension across possible worlds. The alternative view is a sort of giant regularity theory. The truth is true in each world, and *because* of this it is necessarily true. The direction of explanation here seems quite wrong. If this is accepted, the attraction of a metaphysics that treats possible worlds as genuine other worlds is sharply reduced. We will start to look instead for this-worldly truthmakers for necessary truths.

Extensional accounts of necessary truths, of properties and of many another entity have gained their popularity, as I suppose, in part because of the dominance of set theory in our present philosophical culture. But only in part: there is a deeper psychological explanation. The human mind seems to be very comfortable with extensional ways of thinking. Intensional thinking does not come naturally. (Think of the attraction of the Venn diagrams in grasping the propositions of the old formal logic.)[1] Possible worlds, I suppose, are no more than extensional, and therefore fictional, *models* of an intensional reality. But in philosophy we need every crutch that we can find, and we do find it easier to work on many problems involving modality by using extensional models. (False models can be useful. Consider, for instance, the undoubted heuristic value in thinking of the genes as selfish replicators, selfishly seeking to maximize, to reinstantiate, copies of themselves. There may be dangers in this, as some have argued, but the gains, I think, are here well worth the risk.) We need a theory of fiction, of course, and I have no particular suggestions for such a theory, apart from the desideratum that fictions be no more than entities that fail to correspond to reality. Fictions must be propositions, or something similar, and they must lack truthmakers. So I have no wish to ban *talk* of possible worlds, and I do myself talk in this way from time to time. But if we lean to an intensional account of necessity, convinced by a Euthyphro argument or some other consideration, and if we are engaged in seeking truthmakers for necessary truths, then it will be natural to seek for *this-worldly* truthmakers for these truths.

8.2. NECESSARY STATES OF AFFAIRS IN THE RATIONAL SCIENCES?

For most contingent truths, it would seem that the natural truthmakers are contingent states of affairs. If that is so, why should we not postulate

---

[1] An interesting further application of this point is to be found in Gerd Gigerenzer's *Reckoning with Risk* (2002). He shows conclusively how badly we reason when we consider statistical statements by considering probabilities, reasoning that becomes hugely easier if we use natural frequencies, such as frequency in 1,000 cases. That is to say, we do best if we reason extensionally about probabilities.

necessary states of affairs in the world as truthmakers for necessary truths? It is an agreeably simple hypothesis. But, it seems, there is a great stumbling block. The difficulty for this proposal lies in the fact that far the greater part of our knowledge of necessary truth is reached by *a priori* reasoning.

Consider the rational sciences: mathematics, logic and set theory. Whatever we say about the epistemically prior truths in these disciplines (meaning by 'epistemically prior' the ones that we begin with in our investigations), it is undeniable that the necessary truths that we go on to reach from these starting points are arrived at by giving *proofs*. (There is an exception: axioms that are postulated as 'lying behind' our more commonsensical starting points, axioms from which the *epistemic* starting points can be deduced. These recommend themselves not so much by their obviousness, which they may or may not have, but rather by the superior attractiveness of the resulting deductive structure. Russell, I think, made this clear to us. See, in particular, Hager, 1994.)

Furthermore, proof in this context is an operation that is independent, or almost completely independent, of observation and experiment. I do not wish to affirm, it would be a mistake to affirm, that our *a priori* reasoning in these fields leads to logically indubitable knowledge. There is no such knowledge anywhere. But our advanced knowledge in mathematics, logic and set theory is arrived at by thought and calculation alone, now often done on computers as opposed to in our heads, and is *in this sense* not beholden to experience. In these fields there is *proof*. Alleged proofs are not always sound, but we have, in general at least, reliable techniques for checking putative proofs. Granting this, proof has permitted an amazing extension of knowledge in these rightly named 'rational sciences'. This knowledge is not based on observation and experiment. In this sense, it is *a priori* knowledge.

As a result, a close relative of a Kantian epistemological question arises. Suppose that the truthmaker for these different necessary truths is constituted by a number of necessary states of affairs. How is it possible that the mind of the logician or mathematician is able so confidently to grasp the existence of these states of affairs? How is such *a priori* knowledge possible? A doctrine of innate knowledge, with some added guarantee, such as a supernatural guarantee that it is *knowledge*, might do the trick. Let us concede this, at least for the sake of argument. Some philosophers may even argue from the existence of this knowledge to some such conclusion. But suppose that we wish to accept, as I accept, the hypothesis of a naturalist ontology and with it a naturalist epistemology. Then, I submit, it becomes pretty well impossible to understand how the human mind (or, more accurately, certain human minds) can attain to this *a priori* assurance of the existence of all these necessary states of affairs.

So what is to be done? I do not want to retreat to the view that these necessary truths, unlike contingent truths, lack truthmakers or, what is practically equivalent, that all have the very same truthmakers. Nevertheless, what seems to be required, as many empiricist philosophers have thought, is a more or less *deflationary* account of these truths. (Even Kant's own solution to the problem of synthetic *a priori* knowledge is a form of deflationary hypothesis, even if a very unsatisfactory one. We can know these necessities, he argues, only because we ourselves have somehow placed them there. Why, one may ask Kant, does that assure us that we know them? After all, our own mental operations are not transparent to ourselves.) Given a deflationary account, we may be able to answer, or begin to answer, the question how *a priori* knowledge of necessary truths is possible. This for us translates into a deflationary account of the *truthmakers* of these truths.

The deflationary account that I now suggest contains two steps. First it is argued that necessary truths require only *objects* as their truthmakers, as opposed to those proposition-like entities: states of affairs. With this in place, a *Possibilist* account of both the truths and entities of mathematics and logic is defended.

We are to think of <7 + 5 = 12>, to take that as our example, as asserting the existence of a relation between three entities: 7, 5 and 12. Bracket for the moment any question about what numbers are, that is, bracket any question about the ontology of the numbers themselves. Abstracting from its terms, the relation is:

$$(_-+_-) = \; _-$$

It holds for the particular case where 7 and 5 are the first two terms, and 12 the third term. The relation is an internal one. Given the entities 7, 5 and 12, then they must, necessarily must, be related in this way. (Of course, they will be necessarily related mathematically in many other ways also.) Suppose, then, that there are truthmakers for the existence of the entities 7, 5 and 12. These truthmakers will, in turn, necessitate that that relation holds, that is, will necessitate the truth of $7 + 5 = 12$. We can then use a form of the Entailment principle. We have truthmakers for the existence of the three entities (we are supposing). Given the three entities, then the relation must hold. So truthmakers for the existence of the entities should be a sufficient truthmaker for the necessary truth. Although necessary states of affairs are not ruled out by this suggestion, the necessity for postulating them seems removed.

The situation remains the same if the necessary truth is a predication rather than a relation. Consider the truth <7 is a prime number>. Given the number 7 and the property of *being prime*, then the truth is necessitated. This entity and this property, then, can serve as truthmakers for the truth. A predicative tie is not required. All we need are truthmakers for the existence of the number and the property.

Here then is a hypothesis about the truthmakers for necessary truths. Their truthmakers are the entities, whatever they are – they will be very various – which are involved in the truths. These, and these alone, will be the truthmakers for necessary truths. Just by itself, this view does still leave it open that the truthmaking entities are themselves necessary beings and then are truthmakers for necessary truths of the form 'Entity X exists.' Even this hypothesis, however, is one I wish to resist. That will be the work of the next two sections, 8.4 in particular.

8.3. INTERPOLATION: TRUTHMAKERS FOR 7, 5, 12 ETC.

Although this section is something of an interpolation, it will emerge that the conclusion drawn is, at a certain point, a quite important premise for the main argument.

The necessary truth <7 + 5 = 12> has as its truthmakers the natural numbers 7, 5 and 12, or so we have argued. But what is the status of these numbers? What are the truthmakers for the existence of these numbers? A truth such as <the number 7 exists> appears to be a necessary truth. What is its truthmaker? Do we require the necessary existent: the Seven? We must leave the details of this matter to the next chapter, but a preliminary survey here will be useful.

Three answers to the question 'what sort of thing is 7?' come up for consideration. The first is the Platonic answer: 7 is a mathematical entity existing 'outside' – more precisely as something extra to, and independent of – the spatiotemporal world.

The second answer is an intensional, but more down to earth, answer: 7 is some sort of *property* of things. We will not here enquire what sort of property it is – that is left for the next chapter – but since 7 is a natural number it is presumably a property of certain classes and/or mereological wholes. If one accepts universals, it will be natural to think that 7 is a universal, but if one favours tropes, each assemblage of seven entities will have its own sevenness. These wholes will in the first instance be wholes of physical objects or processes of various sorts, but once given the *sevening* property, it can be a constituent of further mathematical structures, such as the square of 7, that involve this property.

The third answer is the extensional answer, the famous Russell–Whitehead answer, that 7 is a class of classes, a class of all those classes that are similar to (can be put in one-one correspondence with) a given class. The given class is one of those classes that, on the *intensional* view, has the property 7.

My idea, of course, would be to reject both Platonism and extensionalism in favour of intensionalism. Like the French aristocrats after Louis XIV had herded them into Versailles, a Platonic realm of numbers standing alongside the physical realm combines ontological extravagance with causal impotence. Whatever was the case in the political analogy, the guillotine – Occam's razor – seems appropriate enough here. The third position, extensionalism, appears to fall to the usual Euthyphro argument. It is natural to think that a certain class of seven things belongs to the class of the classes of seven things in virtue of something about the individual classes, rather than deriving its number from its membership of the class of classes having just seven members. If we accept the intensional answer, as I suggest that we should, there is, of course, still the status of classes to consider. But I deny that they stand apart from ordinary spatiotemporal reality. See the next chapter.

8.4. TRUTHMAKERS FOR TRUTHS OF NECESSITY IN THE RATIONAL SCIENCES

We come now to the second step of this argument, the defence of a Possibilist account of the entities involved. I have claimed that for these sorts of necessary truths the sufficient truthmakers are the entities that the necessary truth links together in some way. But are these truthmakers really *minimal*? Would it not be enough that the entities involved are *possible*? The attraction of this is that we have already seen in chapter 7 that truths of possibility can be supplied with satisfactory truthmakers, that is, relevant truthmakers, at little ontological cost.

In defence of this Possibilist account, we may observe that necessary truths in general (though only in general) are *hypothetical* in nature. They regularly have an 'if...then' form, or may be translated into this form without loss of meaning. We say '7 + 5 = 12', but this can be rendered more transparently, though more boringly, as <necessarily, if there are seven things and five further things, then the sum of these things are twelve things>. Again, colour incompatibilities can best be put in such a form as <necessarily, if a surface is red all over, then it is not simultaneously green all over> (assuming for the sake of the example that the latter proposition is both true and necessary). What are the truthmakers for these hypothetical and necessary truths? These, as already argued, will in the first place be the objects picked out by the truths, such things as numbers, classes, red surfaces and green surfaces. But where the necessary truths are hypothetical, why do we need truthmakers for anything more than the *possibility* of these objects?

It is true that within mathematics and logic, practitioners are accustomed to assert the existence of any entity whose necessary mathematical properties and relations they investigate. These existence claims are not hypothetical in form. This leads to no particular trouble for my account when they are dealing with fairly mundane objects such as intersecting circles. But the realm of the infinite, in particular, leads to serious trouble, at any rate for one looking, as I am looking, for a metaphysics compatible with the view that the world of space-time is all that there is. We know from the work of Cantor that, using his beautiful diagonal argument, the existence of an infinite procession of transfinite cardinals can be demonstrated, each larger than its predecessor in the diagonalizing process. It seems likely that at some finite point in the process an infinite number will be reached such that it is a greater number than the greatest number of entities to be found in space-time, that is, in nature. This may not be the case, but surely it is epistemically plausible. If all these infinite numbers, the infinite cardinals that are *not* instantiated, exist then they must exist independently of space-time. There is still worse to contemplate. The Kantian question, 'How is our knowledge of these entities possible?' (for knowledge it surely is, and *a priori* knowledge at that) returns with the greatest force. Contemporary empiricists, at least, will have a hard time answering this question.

Notice that set theory, which can also be used to enforce the case for indefinite pluralities of entities because of its iterative hierarchy that yields infinity, only compounds the Kantian problem, the epistemic problem that we are considering.

Possibilism solves this problem.[2] Suppose we take it that mathematics and set theory, if the latter is not counted as part of mathematics, deals with structures, very abstract[3] and topic-neutral structures. The infinite numbers are structures of this sort, and so is the set-theoretical hierarchy. What these theorists have discovered, I suggest, is not a whole lot of new entities, to be added to the catalogue of entities in the world, but rather the possibility, the non-self-contradictory nature, of the instantiation of a certain abstract structure. And once we see this, we see that some of these entities may be *mere* possibilities. I will not say more here, but try to say a bit more (within the limits of my competence) in the next chapter that will deal, not at very great length, with number and with classes.

It will be seen, though, how important it was to reject the so-called Platonic view of these entities. It is because infinite numbers, and so forth, are structures potentially instantiated by more ordinary entities, by the sorts of things found in space-time, that we are able to understand the suggestion that some of these structures are merely possible structures. For instance, we can introduce the smallest infinite number, the number of the natural numbers, in the following way. Suppose that there exists a class of Xs having some finite natural number N. Suppose further that, for all N, there exists a class of Xs that has members to the number $N + 1$. If this is true, then the class of the Xs contains at least a denumerable infinity of members. (It will be noted, by the way, that this analysis contains the word 'all', and so if it is true that the number of the Xs is at least the number of the natural numbers, then a general fact, a totality state of affairs, may be involved.)

I submit that, if what I have said here is true, this will greatly ease the problem of truthmakers for these sorts of necessary truth. There may be something mechanical, something purely conceptual, purely semantic, in the deductive following-out of proofs of the existence of the possible.[4] (See the account of analytic truth to come in 8.9.) And where we are dealing with hypothetical truths, and if the question whether or no the terms of the hypothetical truths are truths about actual entities is of no

---

[2] Possibilism has been defended, with a great deal of technical discussion to which I am not able to contribute, by Hilary Putnam (1975) and Geoffrey Hellman (1989). Hellman speaks of 'modalism', but for the purposes of metaphysics 'Possibilism' seems a more transparent name.

[3] Contemporary philosophers generally mean by 'abstract' an entity that is outside space-time. I am using the word in a more ordinary sense. See the *Shorter Oxford Dictionary*: 'To separate in mental conception; to consider apart from the concrete'.

[4] Which is not in any way to denigrate the genius that may be involved in *discovering* proofs.

specifically mathematical or logical concern, and if finally we accept the deflationary truthmakers I have given at the beginning of chapter 7 for truths of mere possibility, then I think the Kantian question has been very largely answered. Long live empiricism – though, admittedly, an ontological purge of a fairly severe sort has had to be undertaken in order that empiricism may survive.

8.5. A DEEPER HYPOTHESIS

I will in this section develop a speculative thesis which, if true, would seem to more or less nail down the step where I argue for the ontological innocence of the relations involved in the necessary truths found in the rational sciences and elsewhere. I will then consider the views of Herbert Hochberg, who thinks that even if my speculative thesis is correct, I am still not home, hosed and dry (8.6). A section, relevant to this dispute, on the important topic of 'internal properties' follows (8.7). Finally I consider truths of impossibility (8.8) and go on to show that difficulties about the notion of analytic truth are rather simply and spectacularly cleared up by drawing the truth/truthmaker distinction (8.9).

Necessary truths are regularly a matter of internal relations holding between the terms of the relation. I have argued at length elsewhere (1997, ch. 10) for the thesis that internal relations are always a matter of an *identity* (and/or *diversity*) holding between the entities that are internally related (identity of particulars or identity of universals). The identity will often take the form of *partial* identity (which is automatically partial diversity), where one entity contains another with something to spare, or else where entities overlap each other. Defence of the notion of partial identity is also to be found in the same work (1997, 2.3.2). This hypothesis about internal relations is certainly controversial and a thorough defence of it requires a lengthy discussion of all sorts of difficult cases, of which the colour incompatibilities are only one of the most notorious. I cannot go through all this material here. I will just say that the strategy used against the difficult cases is two-pronged. Where a case can be made out for identity, including partial identity, such a case is made out. Extensive quantities, such as length and mass, are the particularly plausible cases. Where the identity thesis seems to fail, it is argued that the truths involved are not really necessary after all. A case of the latter is the apparent truth <if *a* is before *b* (in time), then *b* cannot be before *a*>, which is difficult to reconcile with the identity/diversity thesis. I argue (1997, ch. 9) that this proposition

103

may be true, but is not necessary, because the genuine circularity of time (something different from eternal return) is a metaphysical possibility.

This reduction of internal relations to relations of identity and diversity would seem to make rather plausible a deflationary account of internal relations. It is very plausible that mere identity and diversity is a relation that is nothing over and above the related terms. However, all that the present argument requires is the ontological innocence of internal relations. The only truthmakers required are their terms. At the same time, though, if there are falsifiers of the identity/diversity account of internal relations, that *may* reinstate a claim on behalf of these falsifying cases, the claim that necessary states of affairs are required as truthmakers for them. So a good deal may turn on the identity/diversity thesis.

8.6. HOCHBERG ON IDENTITY AND DIVERSITY

Herbert Hochberg, however, has criticized my account of the relations of identity and diversity (see his 1999, pp. 50–1). Hochberg mentions that my view that *a* is the truthmaker for the truth <*a* is identical with itself>, and *a* and *b* are the truthmakers for the truth <*a* and *b* are diverse>, was a view also held by his teacher Gustav Bergmann (1992, pp. 74, 104). (Bergmann, he also reports on p. 46, made the interesting suggestion that it is *diversity* that is the basic relation here, while identity is just the negation of diversity.)

Hochberg, however, argues that 'it is the existence of *a and of b*, where the "and" carries the sense that *a* is diverse from *b*' (1999, p. 50). I find this a weak argument. I agree that this is the function of the word 'and'. It would certainly be odd, knowing what we know, to speak of the morning *and* the evening star (except when asserting their identity). This establishes that diversity is a relation *of some sort*. But it is an internal relation, as I define 'internal', and I see no argument in what Hochberg says to show that the truthmakers for the holding of the relation are anything more than *a* + *b*, where the '+' is the mereological '+', which I further take to be ontologically empty. I know no way to *prove* the point, but I think Hochberg has not proved the contrary. General ontological considerations, plus a certain respect for the Razor, then incline me to give this truthmaker (to a degree deflationary) for the holding of the relation of diversity. Similar remarks apply to identity.

Hochberg is sympathetic to the notion of truthmakers, and speaks of truthmakers quite often in the course of his book. But perhaps he has not fully taken to heart the lack of one-one correlation between truthmakers and truths, and the general possibility that our forms of expression may not automatically give a good 'picture' of the truthmakers that make a truth true. When object *a* is one thing, and *b* is another, then 'diverse from' in '*a* is diverse from *b*' is certainly a two-place predicate, and so *suggests* the linking of *a* and *b* by a further relation. But we are not compelled to think the ontology must go that way, and indeed, I would say, have quite good reasons to think that here the linguistic and ontological structures fail to mirror each other.

8.7. INTERNAL PROPERTIES

Now, though, we come upon a whole series of cases that may seem to force us towards necessary states of affairs. The phrase 'internal properties' is found in the *Tractatus* (see 4.123). (The phrase 'categorial properties' is also in use, but is perhaps too easily confused with 'categorical', so let us instead say 'internal'). The properties we are interested are ones that certain entities have necessarily, where the term 'internal property' nicely complements 'internal relation', the latter covering cases where diverse objects stand of necessity in certain relations.

Thus: universals are not merely the particular universals that they are, but each of them appears to have the property of *being a universal*. (And all tropes may appear to have the property of *being a trope*.) It may seem, indeed, that *being a universal* must be a universal, or *being a trope* must be a trope. Universals, to stick with them, are simple or they are complex, and, it seems, simple or complex of necessity. Again, considering all the mass-universals – the ounce, the kilo, the ton – it is quite plausible to say that all these have a common property: the property of massiness, as we might put it – a *determinable*, to use the technical term – and have this property necessarily. Relation universals have all sorts of formal properties: they are dyadic, triadic and so on. Again, they are symmetrical, asymmetrical, non-symmetrical and so on. These properties would seem to attach of necessity. Will we not be forced to postulate necessary states of affairs?

A case of considerable interest is particularity. I, in common with a good many philosophers, reject the view that particulars are just bundles of properties. The particularity of particulars is irreducible, I think. Suppose this to be so, at least for the sake of argument. I have spoken of the particularity of a particular, abstracted from its properties, as the 'thin' particular. (Bergmann, 1967, pp. 24–5, and his followers spoke of the 'bare' particular. This is an unfortunate piece of terminology in my view, because it suggests the possibility of the existence of particulars in independence of the universals they instantiate, which, I take it, would be a false abstraction.)

But now consider the 'bare' or 'thin' particular. Bergmann, as reported by Hochberg, saw the following problem. 'All bare particulars shared a common feature in that they were all instances of *particularity* . . . Thus they had natures' (Hochberg, 1999, p. 68). At the same time, particulars are supposed to *particularize*, to individuate, to mark off one particular from another. '[Bergmann] . . . thus took a bare particular to be a composite of the categorial universal and an individuating component, and sought to construe these in such a way as to avoid the obvious threatening regress' (p. 69).

The problem of regresses is indeed the problem facing many accounts, or at any rate many realist accounts, of internal properties. A universal may be said to fall under the second-level property of *being a universal*. Does not this property, if it really is an objective property of universals, demand a third-level property of *being a second-level property*? The ensuing regress is not apparently a vicious one, but it does seem viciously uneconomical. If the regress is supposed to halt at the property *being a universal*, then the question arises why even this property is to be admitted. *Predicates* that apply truly can of course be admitted, but perhaps the truthmakers for their true application are in all cases the individual universals. The predicates may ascend, but not the reality in virtue of which they apply.

It must be confessed, though, that it looks very plausible to say that all universals have something objectively in common: *being a universal* looks like a genuine common feature (as does *being a particular*). Might we not therefore admit *being a universal* as a universal, necessarily instantiated by all universals, and give over application of the further 'properties' in the regress to mere predicates? Similarly might we not admit *being a particular* as a property necessarily instantiated by all particulars?

All this reasoning in the case of the internal properties may seem to necessitate accepting certain necessary states of affairs among our truth-makers. I suggest, however, that we may begin to finesse this problem in the same sort of way as that mentioned at the end of 4.5. There, discussing predications about first-order particulars, I suggested that the truth <particular *a* instantiates universal F> is necessary, but that one can still argue that entities *a* and F are contingent existences. (In particular, universals are contingent beings just as much as particulars are.) I have also argued at 7.4 that truthmakers can be given for <there might have been

no contingent beings>. So, there are universals (as I suppose), but there might have been no universals.

Suppose, then, that it is true, as I incline to believe, that <universal U has the property of *being a universal*>. We can accept, we should accept, that this is a necessary truth. But we do not have to accept that there is a necessary state of affairs *U's being a universal* as its truthmaker. Rather, this state of affairs is a *contingent* state of affairs, because the two universals U and the higher-order universal *being a universal* are both *contingent* beings.

But isn't it *conceptually* true that U has the property of being a universal, and does that not set it apart from ordinary first-order predications? No. What is conceptually true is that the *predicate* 'universal' is true of, applies to, U. It is a further step, a metaphysical step, even if as I think a plausible step for a believer in universals to take, that there is a universal of universality. Similar treatment may be possible for other cases of 'internal properties', but this is more a matter for an essay on universals than one on truthmakers. My plea, whatever conclusions are drawn, is to control the metaphysical discussion by continual reference to suggested truthmakers.

8.8. TRUTHS OF IMPOSSIBILITY

We are in this section concerned with truths that record the impossibility of something or other, where that impossibility is absolute. We may begin with the law of non-contradiction <it is impossible for p and not-p both to be true>. We have already, in effect, dealt with the case when we noted (2.4) that the truthmaker for any proposition is simultaneously a falsemaker for the contradictory of that proposition. In the case of an impossible conjunction having the form p & not-p, it is the very same entity (collection of entities) in the world that acts both as truthmaker for one conjunct and falsemaker for the other.

Consider also excluded middle, for those cases where we think that it holds. Given excluded middle, the law excludes the F-F line in the truthtable for p & not-p. Suppose that p is false. It will have a falsemaker. This same entity will be a truthmaker for not-p, thus making it untrue that *both* conjuncts are false.

In the case of the law of non-contradiction there are a few philosophers (mostly in Australia, it has to be admitted) who hold that some substitution-instances of p & not-p are *true*. I do not accept this view, but not a great deal here turns on the point. Truthmaker theory is not in the business of telling us what the truths of logic are, or indeed the truths of any other discipline. What truthmaker theorizing does is search for plausible truthmakers for what are assumed to be truths. Logicians, like others, differ about what propositions are true in their particular subject. I proceed on the assumption that non-contradiction holds for all values. But nothing I have said here is supposed to be any argument for that assumption.

It is, though, interesting to consider what paraconsistentists such as Graham Priest should say if they wanted to embrace truthmaker theory also. Presumably they should say in the cases where non-contradiction breaks down that both *p* and not-*p* have truthmakers. But should it be said that the two sets of truthmakers are identical, or merely overlap, or are disjoint? I do not know what the answer to this is. But if there is no coherent answer to this question, then paraconsistentism and truthmaker theory may be in some conflict.

The conjunction <*p* & not-*p*> is a formal contradiction. The conjunction <this surface is red all over and, at the same time, is green all over> is not. Philosophers have generally accounted this a metaphysical impossibility, but some have denied this. Again, mere truthmaker theory takes no stand on the point. What truths there are, and what their modal status is, is to be determined outside truthmaker theory, in general at least. But let us suppose, for the sake of argument, that the colour incompatibilities are not contingent – that they are metaphysical impossibilities. Then we have much the same truthmaking structure that we found for *p* & not-*p*. If, for instance, <this surface is red all over at time t> has truthmakers, then these truthmakers will be falsemakers for <this surface is green all over at time t>, and vice versa. If, however, it is true that the surface is *neither* red *nor* green all over at this time, then the truthmakers for this truth will be the falsemakers for these two propositions.

The colour incompatibilities, if they are necessary, as I incline to think they are, belong to a (relatively small) class of what we may call *non-transparent* necessities. The contrast is with logico-mathematical necessities, analytic necessities and, if a theory of irreducible and deterministic *powers* in nature is accepted, the necessity of the manifestation of the powers of objects and systems in suitable circumstances. All these necessities are transparent enough. The truthmakers for the colour incompatibilities are, of course, the colours themselves. But the truthmaker structure that lies behind these necessities remains somewhat more mysterious and controversial. My own hope is that physicalist reductions of the secondary qualities will transform the untransparent structure into a transparent one.

A final suggestion. Going beyond truths of impossibility, what of true statements that something is *nonsense*? Thus consider <it is nonsense that quadruplicity drinks procrastination>. This seems to be true. Even here there seems a place for truthmakers, and non-semantic truthmakers at that. Is not this truth true in virtue of what *quadruplicity*, *drinking* and *procrastination* are? There is no call for semantic ascent.

8.9. ANALYTIC AND CONCEPTUAL NECESSITIES

Analytic statements are a species of necessary truth. A traditional view, which has many supporters, is that such truths are true solely in virtue of the meanings of the terms in which they are expressed. At the same time, it is, surely rightly, denied that analytic truths are truths *about* words. <A father is a male parent> is true solely in virtue of the meaning of these terms, in particular 'father' and 'male parent'. But the truth is a truth about *fathers*, not about 'father'.

There is always a certain uneasiness about this solution, a half-feeling that if the statement is true in virtue of words, then it ought to be *about* words. I suggest that truthmaker theory is in a position to dispel this uneasiness. The phrase 'in virtue of' inevitably suggests truthmakers, at least to those attracted to truthmaker theory. So try this. The statement is about fathers. But this particular truth about fathers has as its *truthmakers* nothing but the meanings of the words in which it is expressed. In particular 'father' and 'male parent' have *the very same meaning*. Provided that we do not accept Quinean scepticism about the notion of meaning and sameness of meaning, and for myself I do reject such scepticism, then uneasiness ought to be considerably allayed. Reference is one thing, truthmaking another. The words in which an analytic truth is expressed do not, save *per accidens*, refer to meanings. But the meanings may still be *truthmakers* for the truth. A useful thought here is that given all the meanings, all the analytic truths are fixed. There is supervenience of analytic truth (and indeed analytic falsity) upon meanings. (We can, and should, bracket here the difficult question what meanings *are*, though I would hope for a naturalistic account of meanings.)

So truthmaker theory seems to validate the notion of analyticity (unless we are sceptics about meanings, which I am not). Just how far the domain of analytic truth extends, though, is not for truthmaking theory, *qua* truthmaking theory, to say. But the notion is there for the use of metaphysicians if they see legitimate occasion for such use. That is what this piece of truthmaker theory seems to tell us.

The points made about analytic truths would seem also to apply to conceptual truths. (For some perhaps there is no serious distinction to be made here, though I incline to the view that there is. One consideration that moves me is that other animals – the higher mammals in particular – seem clearly to have certain concepts although they lack language.) Conceptual truths are truths about the intentional objects of the concepts involved. But the truthmakers for these truths are the concepts themselves.

We can thus, I think, use truthmaker theory to make clearer the notion of analytic and conceptual truth. How large is the domain of analytic and/or conceptual truths is a further matter, as I have said. But I have some sympathy with the idea that the truths of the rational sciences, mathematics and logic, are to be accounted analytic or, perhaps better, conceptual. This would, roughly at least, correspond to the views of the early Wittgenstein and the later Russell. There would seem also to be some philosophical propositions that are conceptual truths. The idea of 'conceptual analysis', thought by some in the high days in Oxford to be the only task of philosophy (a position I would reject), seems to have some bite in it, though it is hard to decide how much.

A final note. In the last chapter of his book *Vagueness and Contradiction* (2001), Roy Sorensen argues that certain groups of sentences (I would prefer to say propositions) taken together constitute a refutation of Truthmaker Maximalism – the doctrine that every truth has a truthmaker. These sentences are what he calls 'epistemic islands': the truth of one member of the group depends on the truth of another, but the truth of the other depends, perhaps after going round a circle, on the truth of the first member. There are no truthmakers external to the group, and so, he argues, no truthmakers at all.

For instance, he asks us to consider a list, A, which consists of two identical sentences:

The sentences on list A have the same truth-value.
The sentences on list A have the same truth-value.

The assignments of T-F, F-T, F-F lead to an inconsistency. 'So if the sentences have any truth-value, T-T must be the correct assignment' (2001, p. 167).

I think that we can uphold T-T yet still provide a truthmaker, provided that this result, recast as a rather complex proposition (beginning with

'The sentences on list A...' and ending with 'T-T must be the correct assignment'), constitutes an *analytic* or *conceptual* truth. That, I suggest, is a not implausible contention. The truthmaker will then, as I've argued, be the meaning of the sentences in which this proposition is expressed.

8.10. SUMMING UP

The argument of the two chapters on modality has not been easy. Let us try to get the main points into focus. Truthmakers for truths of mere possibility, it was suggested, may be come upon without too much difficulty. If p is possible, though false, then $<\neg p>$ is a contingent truth. If every contingent truth has a truthmaker (as I maintain), then this truth will have a truthmaker. Given that it is contingent, it necessitates the possibility of p. So why should not the truthmaker for $<\neg p>$, whatever it is, also be the truthmaker for $<\Diamond p>$? This is the Possibility principle. Considerations of coherence, I submit, suggest this getting of such an attractive result for truthmakers of truths of possibility is *itself* a reason for holding that every contingent truth has indeed a truthmaker.

Truths of necessity are not quite so easily dealt with. It is not so clear that the somewhat deflationary result argued for in connection with truths of possibility can be achieved for all classes of necessary truth. Perhaps this can be done in the case of the rational sciences of mathematics and logic. (If some deflationary result cannot be achieved, we empiricists have a serious epistemological problem on our hands.) The suggestion was that the truthmakers for mathematical and logical necessities are the entities (numbers, logical constants and so on) that figure in these truths. As for the existence of these entities I suggested that we embrace Possibilism. It is enough that the instantiation in nature of such things as transfinite numbers be possible rather than actual. If we countenance such things as properties – universals or tropes – we may go on to require necessary truths that predicate properties of these properties. But if truly predicating universals of first-order particulars is necessary, as I now incline to believe, then it can be argued that there is no special problem with these necessities. It was suggested further that although analytic truths are not about meanings, nevertheless their *truthmakers* are to be found in the meanings of the words in which they are stated. The same holds for conceptual truths.

9

Numbers and classes

9.1. INTRODUCTION

Providing truthmakers for the truths of mathematics and set theory (mathematics for short) is an important task for metaphysicians. The demand I place on such truthmakers is that they be compatible with naturalism, defined as the hypothesis that the world of space-time is all that there is. I very much doubt that naturalism is a necessary truth – after all, is not the existence of space-time a contingent matter? But I do think it is a true proposition. The truthmaker for this truth <space-time is all that there is> will be the space-time system itself together with the 'closure' state of affairs that this system is all there is. The deep structure, and the extent, of space-time are of course to be sought by science. The 'manifest image' of space-time is extremely unlikely to be the last scientific word. But I do have a metaphysical hypothesis of a very abstract sort: that the ultimate nature of space-time is a structure of states of affairs (argued for in my 1997).

If the truths of mathematics do not require truthmakers then my task will be eased. I have, however, committed myself to Truthmaker Maximalism: every truth has a truthmaker. So I must find truthmakers for the truths of mathematics in the space-time system. One thought has special influence here. We do not know whether space-time is finite or infinite. It may involve 'structures all the way down' or there may be atoms. It may be infinitely large, or merely very large but nevertheless finite. But the structures of mathematics and set theory involve infinities. How can they find truthmakers in a space-time that may be finite? This drives me towards the view introduced at 8.4: a *Possibilist* account of number and a Possibilist account of the infinities of set theory.

9.2. TRUTHMAKERS FOR THE EXISTENCE OF NUMBERS

We may distinguish in mathematics between existential truths, which tell us that certain mathematical entities exist, and universally quantified truths, having an 'if... then' form. Our present concern is with the existential truths, and in particular the existence of the natural, rational and real numbers.[1] Let us begin by considering the natural numbers, and take as our example the number 4. What sort of truthmaker should we assign to the truth that this number exists? Let us pick out some quadruple, some group of four things, for instance, four particular human beings, Matthew, Mark, Luke and John. We wish to provide a truthmaker for their quadruplicity.

I have already indicated at 8.2 that I wish to reject a 'Platonic' truthmaker, the Form of 4, and also the extensional Russellian view that 4 is a class of classes, the class of classes similar to the class of the Evangelists, say. Euthyphro considerations seem decisive against the extensional view. The number 4 does not attach to a certain class in virtue of that class being a member of the class of fours. Rather it is because that number attaches to the class of the Evangelists that that class is a member of the class of four-membered classes. Of necessity, every class has a definite number of members, a natural number, whether that number be finite or infinite. But the point to be insisted on here is that this number is a *non*-relational (intrinsic) property of the class in question.

It seems, however, that we get still further illumination about the nature of the natural number 4 if we start from mereological wholes, entities that are simpler than classes. Consider the mereological whole of these four men. The mereological whole, as has already been argued, exists automatically, uninterestingly even, provided only that the four men exist. The four of them, taken together, are the truthmaker for the existence of this whole. This whole would seem to be one of the (very many) *minimal* truthmakers for the truth that there are at least four men. (If we wanted to go on and say, what is false, that there are no more men than these then we will need, in addition, a totality fact: this mereological whole comprises the totality of men.)

What makes this whole a whole of four *men*? It is also four mammals, four human beings, four Evangelists, and innumerable other fours, most of them totally uninteresting. But, let us ask, what makes it four *men*? The suggestion of Peter Forrest and myself (Forrest and Armstrong, 1987) is that it is a *relation* holding between the property *being a man* and the

---

[1] Other sorts of numbers, and other mathematical entities, will have to take care of themselves. I claim no expertise in mathematics or mathematical philosophy. Peter Forrest, however, who played the major role in working out our joint theory of number, has the requisite knowledge.

mereological whole that the four men in question constitute. Contemporary scientific knowledge makes it unlikely that *being a man* is a universal, but it is a property in some more relaxed sense, and it is instantiated four times by the mereological whole. We may say that this mereological whole 'fours' the property of *being a man*. We do need to note that among the innumerable instantiations of the four-relation will be cases where both the property and the mereological whole are purely mathematical entities. Thus, the numbers 5, 6, 7 and 8, themselves relations if this account is correct, constitute a mereological whole that 'fours' *being a natural number*. Hence this whole is truthmaker for the fact that this whole is a whole of four natural numbers. (And, of course, it is a truthmaker for all sorts of other mathematical truths involving just these four numbers.) But having said this about purely mathematical mereological wholes, let us here concentrate upon the cases where the mereological whole involved is a whole of empirical objects.

It is to be noted that the properties that enter into the *four*-relation, though not necessarily universals, are what may be called 'unit-determining properties'. By this is meant that their instances are *ones*, one of that type of entity. Classes, because they have a particular cardinality, are essentially a certain number of *ones*, things that, within the particular class, are taken each as a unit. The properties involved may be thought of as cookie-cutters that cut one instance out of the mereological whole to which they are related. In the case of Matthew and the others, each of the four objects is wholly disjoint from the other three. This is the neatest sort of case. But consider three delineated squares on a uniform background, where one square stands apart and the other two overlap in such a way that the portion of their overlap is also a square (fig. 9.1). Here the four objects, four squares, are not wholly disjoint, but this delineation does 'four' the unit-property of *being a delineated square on this surface*. Contrast properties such as *being red* or *being extended*. These properties do not 'determine a unit'.

What has been said about the nature of classes does not fit the null class, of course. But I suggest that we do not want the null class as an entity. It is not a constituent of the world. It may be useful to introduce it in the formalisms of set theory, but references to it there, I would hope, do not require that there be a thing called the null class which is truthmaker for the strange proposition <there is a class that has no members>. I suggest, instead, that this is not a true proposition of metaphysics.

The number 4, on this account, appears to be an instantiated dyadic universal (complex rather than simple), or, if a trope account of properties

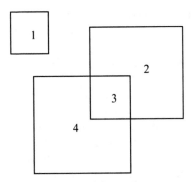

Fig. 9.1. Four delineated squares

and relations is preferred, it is an equivalence class of tropes unified by the equivalence relation of exact similarity. It is very like the totality relation, which also holds between properties broadly conceived and mereological wholes. There is, however, an important difference. For many cases, the totality relation is a contingent one. It is a contingent truth, for instance, that the totality of being, provided it is not described as such, is indeed the totality of being. 'In some other possible worlds' it would not be the totality of being because there was more besides.

Consider, however, Matthew, Mark, Luke and John. It is contingent that they exist, and perhaps it is contingent that they are men. But it is in virtue of their being men – whatever be the truthmaker for the truth that they are men – that their mereological whole stands in the four-relation to the property *being a man*. So, unlike many totality cases, the relation is an internal one. Given the terms of the relation, the relation is necessitated. The relation supervenes upon the terms. Indeed, in the case of the numerical relations it supervenes upon the existence of the second term, the mereological whole. For given that whole, then the corresponding property, whatever its nature, is automatically an existent, because it is found instantiated within the whole. The *being-four-men* property of the whole is a particular sort of *structural* property, a rather simple sort of structural property, of the whole. The whole is a truthmaker for its possession of this property.

But if that is so, then it seems that the truthmaker for the existence of this instantiation of the four-relation is nothing beyond the existence of its terms (the property and the mereological whole). If it is correct to say that the truthmaker necessitates the truth of what it makes true, then the existence of the terms necessitates the relation that holds between them, the four-relation, and so, by transitivity, necessitates the truth that the terms are so related. And since the property (*being a man*) is instantiated *within* the mereological whole, the instantiation is a non-relational (but structural) property of the mereological whole.

It would seem, incidentally, that for internal relations, though not for external relations, the view that relations are very often *ordered* pairs of their relata has a good deal to commend it. Where a pair stands in a fixed relation, one that is fixed, that is, necessitated, by the nature of the pair, there we have an internal relation. If such relations are ordered, the order springs from differences in the terms. A less ontologically economical truthmaker, one that I do not want to postulate, would be a necessary state of affairs that necessitated the truth that the internal relation holds between the pair.

Moving on, Peter Forrest has pointed out (Forrest and Armstrong, 1987, sec. III) that our account of what a natural number is can be generalized with little difficulty to cover the rational and the real numbers. With rational and real numbers, we move into the realm of quantity. The unit-property becomes what may be called a 'unit of measure', and the internal relation that it stands in to its mereological whole is a relation of *proportion*. The unit-property might be *weighing a kilogram*, and it might stand in the $2/3$ proportion to a particular quantity of potatoes. If R is the unit-property, in this case a unit of length, then it stands in the 2π proportion to the length of the circumference of a perfect circle having radius R.

9.3. A PROBLEM FOR THIS ACCOUNT

But now to consider the great problem that arises for this account of these numbers. According to this view, such a number exists if and only if a certain (internal) relation exists between a unit-property and some actual mereological whole. But what of very large numbers, in particular the infinite cardinals? May not the world be finite? If it is, then some of these relations will not be instantiated. And what will be the truthmaker for the truth that such numbers exist?

It may be, of course, epistemically may be, that space-time is mathematically continuous. If so, certain small infinite numbers will be instantiated 'all the way down', in the realm of the small, even if space-time has but a finite extent. But this only asks us to consider infinite numbers that are bigger than the number of the continuum. At some point in the infinite progression of the infinite cardinals, it is likely that the world contains no whole that has that cardinality.

It is here that the truthmaker doctrine forces hard choices upon us. We should, I think, rejoice in these choices rather than turn on the truth-maker doctrine. Philosophy is not meant to be easy. A Platonist will solve the problem by postulating *uninstantiated* numbers (presumably universals rather than tropes). The truthmaker problem is solved, although at con-siderable ontological and, indeed, epistemic cost. Again, if we assume no limitation of size upon worlds, a realist doctrine of possible worlds will al-low for the instantiation of any infinite number. But again the ontological and epistemological cost is great.

My own hard choice, as already indicated in chapter 8, is to accept a deflationary doctrine of what it is for a mathematical entity to exist. Plenty of mathematical structures exist in a straightforward sense, because they are instantiated. We can call them *empirical* mathematical structures. It is the fact that so many interesting and fruitful mathematical structures are empirical (something amazing that could hardly have been foretold *a priori*) that allows science, and in particular physics, to achieve its almost incredible 'mathematizing of nature'. But mathematical existence itself, I suggest, should be reckoned as something less. A mathematical entity exists if and only if it is *possible* that there should be instantiations of that structure. This transforms the question of truthmakers for the existence of mathematical entities into a question of truthmakers for truths about certain *possibilities*.

Truths of possibility are weaker, they say less, than the corresponding truths that assert actuality. (Actuality entails possibility, but possibility does not entail actuality.) We can therefore have good hope, *pace* Platonists, that less will be required in the way of truthmakers for them. They *should* be ontologically less demanding. Furthermore, it may be, as many empiricists have hoped, that at least some necessary truths are also ontologically less demanding. (But probably not all.) We have already seen an example of this in discussing internal relations. Where such relations hold, it is a necessary truth that they hold. But it is, I hope, quite plausible to argue that the truthmakers for these necessary truths are nothing but the existence of the terms of the relation.

I recognize, of course, that asserting here this *Possibilist* doctrine of mathematical existence is to a degree a matter of hand-waving. I have not got the logico-mathematical grasp to defend it in any depth. That has been done, in particular by Geoffrey Hellman (1989). In an earlier draft of this book I said that as far as I know no serious difficulties for the programme have emerged. But it has since been suggested to me that in fact there is at least one serious difficulty to be faced. By good fortune, however, the theory of classes that I put forward in the second half of this chapter contains, as I hope, a prospect of answering the problem. I shall therefore not even state the problem here, but will expound it, together with my answer to it, at the end of this chapter.[2]

But here, immediately, let me re-emphasize the huge problem posed, at least to empiricists, and still more to empiricist/naturalists, by the *a priori* nature of mathematical and logical reasoning. Kant's problem was a real one. What can the truthmakers be for mathematical proofs, and what truthmakers can there be for the existence of the entities whose existence and non-existence mathematics *proves*? Quinean attempts to break down the division between the rational and the empirical sciences, attempts to see the division as a mere difference of degree, seem very implausible. A Possibilist account of the *uninstantiated* logico-mathematical structures looks to be the only plausible programme that might resolve the problem for empiricists.

If this Possibilism is correct, then the whole of mathematics and logic moves in the realm of the possible, for certain cases (perhaps big infinite cardinals), into the realm of the merely possible. Mathematics deals purely with abstract, topic-neutral structures, some of which may be merely possible structures. A deflationary account of truths of mere possibility was offered in chapter 7 – no realm of the merely possible need be postulated as truthmaker for truths of mere possibility. Suppose, for instance, that the world is finite in every respect. The infinite numbers all become non-empirical but possible mathematical structures. And a naturalist such as myself will hold that the *instantiated* structures are all to be found in space-time.

9.4. MANY-MEMBERED CLASSES

We turn our attention to classes. David Lewis (1991) pointed out that many-membered classes are nothing more than *mereological* wholes of the classes formed by taking the singleton of each member:

$$\{a, b, c, d, \dots\} \text{ is identical with } (=) \{a\} + \{b\} + \{c\} + \{d\} + \dots$$

---

[2] It may be noted also that Hellman, as I think, stacks the deck against himself by not recognizing (sparse) properties and relations in his ontology.

As I see it, Lewis has here made an invaluable contribution to the meta-physics of classes. The right-hand side of the identity statement has most elegantly separated out the mereological and non-mereological elements involved in many-membered classes. One important thing that emerges more clearly in the right-hand side is that the class/sub-class relation is nothing but the mereological relation of whole to proper part (symbol-ized by '+'). The right-hand side looks strange and artificial at first sight, but on reflection it can be seen better to bring out (picture, even!) the nature of the class. This can best be appreciated by contrasting the class with the mereological whole associated with it, that is, contrasting it with the mereological sum of its members:

$$a + b + c + d + \ldots$$

This whole (think of it as a rock or something like that) divides into proper parts (it really contains parts, even where the parts are physically inseparable) in innumerable ways, particularly if the parts enumerated are themselves objects with proper parts. Restricting ourselves to just two different ways of dividing up a certain reasonably complex mereological whole, our rock, say, we might have:

$$a + b + c + d = e + f + g + h,$$

but where the parts enumerated here are each of them numerically diverse from all the other seven. In general, there will be innumerable ways to mark off parts which sum to this *one* whole, the rock as it may be. But the associated *classes* that can be formed from these parts are all different classes. Thus:

$\{a + b + c + d\}$ is not identical with $\{e + f + g + h\}$.

One whole, many ways of dividing it up into proper parts. Associated with each of these many ways of dividing there will be a *different* class (fig. 9.2).

It is the dividing up that explains why, in general, there are many classes associated with the one whole, even where all the members of the class are individuals rather than being classes themselves. It will be seen, though, that what I have just said tacitly assumes that for each many-membered class, its members do form a mereological whole. This, it seems to me, is an important reason for accepting the principle of Unrestricted Mereological Composition. That assumption allows us to say that there will always be a mereological whole associated with a class, a whole that is the sum of the members of the class. This will hold however heterogeneous the members

119

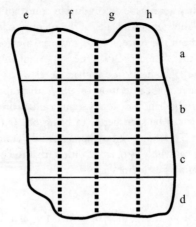

Fig. 9.2. Different ways of subdividing the same mereological whole to give different classes

of the class may be. The Sydney Opera House and $\sqrt{-1}$, as all allow, go happily together in a two-membered class, but they also, I insist, form a mereological whole. At the same time there seems to be no inflation in the ontology. Where parts make up a mereological whole, the whole and its parts supervene on each other. This strongly suggests identity, and identity is ontologically costless.

The *singleton* class-operator $\{x\}$ then becomes, as it were, the means of keeping the parts of classes separate, marking off each member of each class, and so making two classes non-identical even where the mereological sum of the totality of members of these classes is the very same sum.

9.5. SINGLETONS

This, I think, is the beginning of wisdom if we are concerned with the metaphysics of classes. But it brings us face to face with the really hard questions: 'What is a singleton?', 'What is it that gives this extra structure to wholes?', 'What is the proper ontology of singletons?', 'What is the truthmaker for the truth that a certain singleton exists?' Lewis, following on his brilliant insight, proceeds to makes very heavy weather of this, finding singletons mysterious in the extreme. He remains, though, and surely correctly remains, unwilling to jettison set theory, and equally unwilling, again surely correctly, to deny that a and $\{a\}$ are different entities.

I will come very shortly to the reason why singletons are such a difficulty for him.

In past work I have presented my theory as a theory about what singletons *are*. But I now claim no more than that I am giving satisfactory truthmakers for the existence of singletons. That this need not be a mere verbal difference may be seen, for instance, from the case of internal relations. I claim that where a relation is necessitated by its terms, there the terms by themselves (the mereological sum of the terms) are a sufficient truthmaker for the holding of the relation between these terms. Yet it seems wrong to say that this truthmaker constitutes the relation. Just for a start, the same truthmaker might be truthmaker for more than one internal relation. Indeed, it could be claimed with some plausibility that it is a category mistake to identify the relation with the sum of its terms. Yet the terms may still be all that is required by way of *truthmaker* for the internal relation in question.

The first point to make is that any hypothesis about the proper truthmakers for a singleton, or at any rate any hypothesis that will pass muster with an empiricist and naturalist, ought to have the member of the singleton as a constituent. The symbol { ... } is an operator, and, of course, an operator may take what it operates upon to something quite different. The operator 'an uncle of' operating upon Joe takes Joe to quite another person. But if Joe's singleton { ... } takes its member to some other entity, what could that entity be? It does not seem good enough to answer 'Joe's singleton'. Is this supposed to be a new primitive entity? A Platonist about classes might, I suppose, hazard such an answer. But what is there in the space-time world, where I would hope to find all truthmakers, that is wholly distinct from Joe, yet is truthmaker for the existence of Joe's singleton? This truthmaker, though not identical with Joe, must nevertheless be *partially identical* with him. In particular, it must contain Joe together with something more.

This leads to the suggestion that the truthmaker required is some sort of *state of affairs*, a state of affairs that involves Joe. What we need is some property attaching to Joe that marks him off as a *one*, as a *unit*, and so makes him a member of a class. Such a state of affairs will serve as truthmaker for the existence of {Joe}. *Joe's being a human being* will serve nicely. Joe will, of course, have indefinitely many further properties that mark him off as a *one*, and so will be a constituent of indefinitely many other states of affairs. These properties are what I at 9.2 called 'unit-properties'. Since we want to generalize, we can say that whatever states of affairs make Joe a *one* is a truthmaker for Joe's having *unithood*[3] – a 'property' of all these unit-properties. Whether we really need this property of unithood in the ontology, and so as a truthmaker, is a delicate matter about which I am uncertain. But at least we need the unit-properties.

Lewis might have other objections to this line of thought, but there is one objection that is an absolute stumbling block to him. Holding as he did that *all* composition in the world is mereological, he cannot accept the idea that the truthmaker for {*a*} embeds *a* in a state of affairs, because states of affairs, if they exist, have a non-mereological unity. But we have already seen that the postulation of states of affairs solves important problems in truthmaking theory. Singletons become a mystery if all composition is mereological. So the present hypothesis is an attractive one to consider. It does, however, need a modification to make it work, as will be noted shortly.

The idea is that the braces {} attribute to *a* the place-holding, or perhaps determinable, property of *unithood*. A single member of a class is surely a *one* or a *unit*, and to have unithood the member has to have some property which determines the member to be a one – being a pig, or being a patch of red colour, and not just being pork or being red. But, with this allowed, the property can be quite second-rate and/or relational. Different members of the one class must each have unithood, they must be ones, they must be units, of some sort, but may have nothing further in common, although the interesting classes are generally united by resemblances between their members. What we have as truthmaker for each of the singletons involved is a certain sort of state of affairs. States of affairs once more show their ontological value as truthmakers.

9.6. THE ACCOUNT OF SINGLETONS REFINED

I have above identified the truthmaker for a singleton with the embedding of its member in some state of affairs by some property or other of a unit-determining sort. This is too crude and actually leads to a contradiction, as Gideon Rosen demonstrated to my discomfiture (Rosen, 1995). Given iterative set theory that climbs forever up the infinite numbers, it is impossible for every singleton to be a state of affairs. A simple but important case that falsifies my original theory is the case of W, the whole world, the whole that contains absolutely every thing that exists. (Greater than

---

[3] A term suggested to me by David Lewis. It was a characteristic of Lewis to give help, and suggest terminology, even where he lacked sympathy with the theory being advanced.

which nothing exists.) Set theory sees no difficulty in putting W into a singleton {W}, and then erecting the whole of iterative set theory on top of this singleton. But you cannot put W into even one really existing state of affairs. States of affairs are ampliative, that is, they *embed* their subjects in something further. But if W really is *everything*, then there is nothing further, not just no further particulars, but no further properties or relations or anything else. If W is to have a singleton, as it seems that it should have, some quite deflationary account of this singleton will have to be given.

At this point I draw a distinction between empirical and non-empirical classes. Remember the distinction drawn in 9.3 between empirical and non-empirical mathematical structures. The former are mathematical structures that are actually instantiated, the latter, I suggested, are to be put into the class of 'mere possibilities', structures that might have been instantiated, but are in fact not instantiated (omnitemporally, I would say). Now set theory is a matter of producing certain sorts of (very general) mathematical structure. Some of these structures, in general the simpler ones, will be instantiated. The ones that are not instantiated are, on this view, to be ranked among the *mere* possibilities. No matter, then, if actual states of affairs run out in the higher reaches of set theory. Merely possible states of affairs will do.

Thus, consider W. Its singleton must be accounted a non-empirical state of affairs. The world (it would seem, at least) could have been bigger than it is. It is possible that what is in fact W should be a proper part of the true W, W* as we may call it. Then W would have been embedded in various states of affairs. For instance, there might have been extra properties instantiated in W, or relations to extra particulars. That is all we should ask in order for set theory to be entitled to place W in a singleton – that it be non-self-contradictory that W have unithood. Mathematical existence need be no more than the *possibility* of the instantiation of the mathematical structure that is said to exist. So the structure {W} is non-empirical.

Mere possibilities, I argued in 7.2, will have in every case actualities as their truthmakers. It is the case that W is the totality of being (by definition). It is possible that W is not the totality of being. <There might have been W plus something further> is, we may assume, a modal truth. Its truthmaker, I then assert, is the actual totality of being: W. (To gesture at the argument of 7.2: if *p* is contingent it will have a truthmaker, this truthmaker will also be a truthmaker for <not-*p* is possible>, via the Entailment principle.) The truthmakers for singletons, then, are not always states of affairs. They are sometimes the mere possibility of states of affairs.

9.7. A DIFFICULTY FOR POSSIBILISM

I finish this chapter by discussing the serious difficulty that may be thought to face Possibilism about mathematics. Fraser MacBride has urged to me what he calls the problem of modal vacuity:

[the problem of] establishing that it is genuinely possible for the universe to contain as many things as the antecedents of the hypotheticals in a given mathematical theory demand. It is a difficulty because the only serious means we have for establishing such possibility claims appears to be by modeling them in the universe of sets. So it appears (to many) that really our grasp of the space of possibility is mediated by a prior understanding of an actually existing platonic realm of objects (i.e. existing sets).[4]

He gives as a reference Stewart Shapiro (Shapiro, 1997, pp. 88–9, 228–9).

But my suggestion is that we carry through Possibilism to apply in set theory just as much as in the other areas of mathematics. The existence of a mathematical entity according to my Possibilism is no more than the possibility of the instantiation of that sort of structure somewhere in space-time. The empirical structures are those that are actually instantiated, the non-empirical the ones that are nowhere instantiated. The purity of mathematics, on this view, is that it abstracts from instantiation though it does demand the possibility of instantiation. Why may we not extend all this to include set theory? Why should we not distinguish between empirical and non-empirical classes? Consider a very big class, one that has a very big infinite cardinality. It will be plausible to say that the world does not instantiate that structure – there are not that many things in the world – and so that this class is a non-empirical one, one that picks out a *mere* possibility for the world.

It may still be argued that this commits me to a world or worlds of possibilia stretching far beyond the actual world. To this I reply by going back to my treatment of mere possibilities in 7.2. I argued there that a satisfactory truthmaker (not necessarily a minimal truthmaker) for <it is possible that p> is whatever is the truthmaker for the proposition <it is not the case that p>. In the case we are considering, this truth will be that the particular structure envisaged, the class with a very big infinite cardinality, is not to be found in the world. By Truthmaker Maximalism, at least, this true assertion of non-existence will have a truthmaker, though perhaps that truthmaker will be the whole world, W.

---

[4] Private communication, quoted by kind permission.

10

Causes, laws and dispositions

We know that, in innumerable cases, one billiard ball strikes another and causes the latter to move. David Hume, very justly, used this as a paradigm case of causation: one token event causing a further individual event to occur. But given that it is true that a token event C causes a further event E to occur, what is the truthmaker for this truth? What *metaphysics* of causation should we accept?

According to the 'Humean' tradition (I use quotation marks here to distance myself from the scholarly question of what Hume himself actually believed), what makes the individual sequence a causal sequence lies outside that sequence. Considered in abstraction from its spatiotemporal environment, the sequence is neither causal nor not causal. It is in virtue of the right spatiotemporal context that such a sequence is causal. The notion of a cause is *tied* to that of some regularity in nature. Along with the regularity theory of causation goes a regularity theory of laws. A residual problem remains: not all laws of nature seem to be causal laws. (Conservation laws are not implausible candidates.) What marks off causal laws from laws that are not causal? Humeans, however, hardly bother to distinguish them.

It may be added that the counterfactual theory of causality popularized by David Lewis is fundamentally a Humean theory, at any rate as Lewis developed it. For Lewis subscribed to the doctrine of Humean supervenience, the doctrine that, in this world at least,[1] all causes and laws supervene, and supervene without ontological addition, upon particular

---

[1] I say 'in this world at least' because I do not know whether Lewis did, or did not, hold that Humean supervenience holds in every possible world. Again, he might have been agnostic on the question. He would, however, then have condemned worlds where the supervenience fails to hold as rather unsatisfactory worlds!

matters of fact. These particular matters of fact do not, for Lewis, include any singular causal relations or primitive nomic ties between selected properties. Given this, regularities in the world would seem to be the only truthmakers for causal and nomic truths that this world affords. In a wide or loose sense, Lewis is a regularity theorist.

The view that is opposed to regularity theories of causation may be called, often is called, the singularist view. According to this view, which is my own view, the truthmaker for the sequence being causal is the holding of a dyadic relation, the relation of singular causation, between the token events themselves. This relation is, using terminology introduced by Lewis, *intrinsic to its pairs*. (He himself, of course, rejected singular causation in this sense.)

If the relation is intrinsic to its pairs, there is a further question whether the relation holds necessarily or contingently. The orthodox analytic view until recently is that the relation is contingent. But if we admit properties into our ontology, and if furthermore *powers* are an essential component of properties, then we seem to get a necessary connection *in re* holding between token causes and token effects. Again, even if we deny that properties are powers, but do allow them to be universals, causation may come out as necessary. I have said at 4.4 that the attribution of properties to particulars in states of affairs may well be a necessary one. This should hold for polyadic states of affairs as well as monadic ones and also, it seems, for higher-order states of affairs, such as the particular sort of connection between universals that I hold to constitute a law of nature.

In any case, it should be noticed that the dispute between regularity theorists and singularists once again takes the form of a Euthyphro dilemma. Is causation in the singular case to be accounted causation in virtue of the fact that it is an instance of some regularity, or does the regularity exist in virtue of the fact of causation in the singular case? Once again, we have an extensional treatment of a metaphysical issue opposed to an intensional one. The intensional answer is attractive, I think, but as we will now see it can be opposed by another Euthyphro argument that points in the other direction.

10.2. CAUSAL LAWS

The trouble is that we think that there is some very close connection between causes and *laws of nature*. (Notice here that we will be taking 'law of nature' in its *ontological* rather than its propositional sense. We are not concerned with true statements of law, but rather with the truthmakers for such statements.) Causes and laws seem to be intertwined. There may perhaps be laws that do not involve causation (although all natural laws involve the notion of a certain type of thing determining – or probabilifying – something further). But where there are causes, there seem to be laws. From the same causes (same *sort* of cause) we think, in general at least, that the same effects will flow. And this has strong claims to be part of the essence of causation.

Assume now that these claims are true. The answer to the Euthyphro dilemma about causation becomes much less clear. Indeed, as anticipated above, we face a second Euthyphro dilemma, but one that points in the opposite direction. In virtue of what is a particular (token) causal sequence, say event A followed by event B, law-governed? Is the law-governed nature of the sequence an intrinsic property of the sequence, an intrinsic property in virtue of which other As are followed by Bs? Or is it an instance of a law-governed sequence in virtue of the fact that elsewhere the same pattern is found: As being followed by Bs?

At face value, the second answer is far more plausible. Laws, after all, are essentially general. They are usually thought of as holding everywhere in space-time. Even if there could be laws that are 'local' only, that locality will be extremely large, we think, and the law would hold throughout the locality. There are, of course, putative laws that may be called 'defeasible' laws – laws that hold only 'other factors being equal'. But these are still thought of as general: the defeasibility holds across their extension.

So it seems quite plausible to say that the truthmaker for a particular instantiation of the law's being an instantiation of the law lies not in the instantiation itself but in the fact that it an instance of a wider regularity. (Regularities, of course, may demand general facts, general states of affairs, as I have argued following Russell, in chapter 6, but we can bracket that issue in the present context.) Humeanism may seem counterintuitive with respect to causes, but it seems quite intuitive with respect to laws. And if causes actually involve laws, as it is natural to assume, then the apparent need to put the causation into the instance, and the apparent need to put the law-like nature of the causation into the regularity and not the instance, stand in sharp conflict. We have a nasty dilemma on our hands. Thinking in terms of truthmakers only sharpens the dilemma.

More precisely, we can construct a *trilemma*:

(1) Singular causation is a relation 'intrinsic to its pairs'. (Singularism)
(2) Singular causation is essentially law-governed. (Common sense)
(3) Laws are essentially general. (Obvious)

It appears on the surface that it is not possible to accept all three of these theses. Accepting any two of these propositions seems to involve rejecting the third. Yet all three are individually attractive. So let us consider in turn the costs of abandoning one of the three.

We can try abandoning (1), that is, abandoning singularism. That has been the path favoured by English-speaking philosophy ever since Hume. Token causation does give a strong impression that it is a relation intrinsic to its pairs, requiring nothing elsewhere in the world for it to *be* causation. But perhaps that impression can be explained away. Hume himself had an ingenious explanation of why we 'project' causation into the singular case. The perceived regularity works on our mind to pass naturally, in perception or thought, from the token cause to the token effect, and we mistake this mental connection of ideas for a real and intrinsic connection in the token objects. Provided that this mental mechanism can itself be understood as a mere regularity, then the impression of singular causation can be explained away as a natural illusion. The only truthmakers for causal truths are the regularities of the world.

I am very reluctant to take this line, among other reasons because I think there is good reason to think that we perceive singular causality. Using Hume's terminology, but contradicting his doctrine, I believe we have an impression, a sense-impression, of causality, from which the idea (the concept) of causality is derived. I have previously argued this in more detail, particularly in my *A World of States of Affairs* (1997, 14.6: 'The epistemology of singular causation'). The philosophically little-discussed perception of pressure on our own body – in general the action of force on our body – is as directly perceived, I maintain, as anything else in our experience. It is, for instance, as directly perceived as colours or simple spatial relations. (See the excellent and more thorough discussion in Fales, 1990, ch. 1 especially.) But if causality involves nothing but regularities of an extensive sort, it would be impossible that causality should be so directly perceived. How could you non-inferentially perceive cosmic regularities? If one subscribes to a causal theory of perception, as many do and as I do myself, the cosmic regularity would have to be the ultimate cause of the perception of causality in the individual. This seems absurd. We require causal relations holding between singulars as truthmakers for truths of singular causation.

An interesting attempt by a Humean to link singular sequences with laws is to be found in Donald Davidson (1995). He holds that there actually is a conceptual connection between singular causal sequences and laws. Answering a challenge to him put forward by Elizabeth Anscombe (1975), he argues that it is part of our concept of causation that individual cases of causation fall under laws. This holds even where, as usually happens, we are ignorant what the actual law involved is. Laws he treats as a species of true universally quantified proposition, and would perhaps mark the species off from its genus in the style of the Mill–Ramsey–Lewis theory. These truths are for him (I presume) made true by, have as their truthmakers, certain sorts of uniformity. He then links cases of singular causes with laws in the following way. He is a thoroughgoing nominalist about properties and therefore takes Goodman's problem about *grue* very seriously. There is, he argues, a grue-like problem even about what constitutes a real change. We think that a change from green to blue is a real change at the instant of change and is caused, but a change from grue to bleen may not be a real change. Why do we select 'green' and 'blue' as 'good' predicates, worthy to describe real and caused changes in the world, and scorn 'grue' and 'bleen'? (A genuine problem for one who denies objective properties.) We do it, he says, just because the first way of grouping things together produces true and powerful universal generalizations about singular sequences. Singular causation therefore has law written into it.

This is ingenious, and points to something important: that the *identification* of the true properties of things and the laws that they obey go hand in hand. We look for theories in which properties and laws fit smoothly and naturally together. But a devotion to truthmaker theory will lead us to ask just what it is in the world that makes certain universal generalizations 'true and powerful'? I don't think that a nominalist such as Davidson, one who denies the existence of properties *in re*, has the metaphysical resources to answer this question.

Suppose, then, that we wish to stay with genuinely singular causation. What shall we say about (2) – the law-governed nature of singular causation – and (3), that laws are general? It does not seem possible to give up (3). A law, to be a law, must have some actual, or at least potential, generality, even if this generality is in some way restricted, say to certain expanses of space-time or by defeasibility. What about abandoning (2)? The Humean line keeps causes and laws close together, perhaps seeing causes as a particular variety of regularity. But when confronted by the trilemma a singularist might try to drag them apart. One can accept the reality of singular causation, yet still be a Humean about causal *laws*. The operation of singular causation, one might maintain, is regular as a mere matter of fact. It is not an essential feature of causation. It could have been that from the same sort of cause, quite different effects follow on different occasions. That, however, does not in fact happen, and so we are able to predict from the nature of the token cause what effect it will, in general, produce. Perhaps this was the position held by Elizabeth Anscombe (1975). Causes are singular, but regularities in *what causes what* are mere regularities.

I should like to see this halfway position fully worked out, but it makes an unsatisfying impression. A natural response is either to go for a more complete (though no doubt sophisticated) Humeanism about both causes and laws, or else adopt some position that accepts both 'strong' causation (causation as a relation that is 'intrinsic to its token pairs'), and also 'strong laws' (laws that necessitate regularities, but where the mere regularities do not necessitate the laws). I have indicated that I reject Humean accounts of causation. I also reject Humean accounts of laws, and have criticized that view elsewhere at some length. (See in particular my 1983, chs.1–5.) I incline to think that combining a Humeanism about laws with singularism about causes – a position, however, that I did not discuss there – will do little to help Humeanism about laws. But what I will try to do now instead is to show that there is more than one position that can actually straddle the divide between cause and law, the divide that the Euthyphro question *seems* to enforce. The apparently unbridgeable chasm between causes and laws can actually be bridged. The 'trilemma' is not really a trilemma.

The key to getting a theory of genuinely singular causation that is at the same time essentially law-governed causation lies, I believe, in the notion of *property*. If we have (sparse) properties as truthmakers in our ontology, then we can, under the guidance of scientific investigation, attribute properties to the event or state of affairs that is the cause and to the further event that is the effect. *Pace* Davidson, properties will be needed even to get truthmakers for mere Humean laws, mere regularities. How can you get a genuine regularity without genuine cases of 'same thing again'? Universals, or else tropes collected by the equivalence relation of exact similarity, will be required. But if we want to go beyond mere regularities, we will need some *link* between the properties of the cause and the properties of the effect, a linking of the properties that will ensure that from token causes that have the same properties, the same effect will flow. Only so will the causal regularities be *explained*.

We have already seen in chapter 4 that sparse properties can be taken in different ways. Two of the choices are of interest here. They can be taken as universals or as tropes; they can be taken as powers or taken categorically (as qualities). Combinatorially, this gives four positions, all worthy, *prima facie*, of consideration by metaphysicians. It seems that three of these positions, if they can be developed in certain ways, enable us to uphold all the propositions in the alleged trilemma. Quality-tropes, that is, tropes that are not taken as powers, seem to be the only position where there seems no way of evading the trilemma.

10.2.1. Powers to the rescue?

One attractive way of upholding all three propositions in the trilemma is by identifying the true properties of the world with *powers*. It turns out, moreover, that these powers can be conceived of either as universals or as tropes, yet still do what is wanted. I reject theories of this sort, for reasons to be given at 10.4, but they are certainly very worthy of consideration.

Suppose, first, that these power-properties of particulars are universals. Each of these universals bestows certain powers, either singly or in suitable conjunction with further universals, to produce certain outcomes (or to be produced by certain antecedents). Same universal, or universals, automatically gives us the same power, because, given the theory we are considering, the universals are powers. Same universals instantiated in different particulars will then, in the same conditions, *necessarily* yield the same effect (or a certain objective probability of the same effect), which gives us laws that could not be otherwise. Laws supervene on powers on this theory. And since cause and effect are 'distinct existences' – that is a Humean premise that can hardly be rejected – what we have in the world on this view are *necessary connections between wholly distinct existences*. Singular causation and its essentially law-like nature can then be upheld along with the generality that law obviously involves. The laws, though general, are fully instantiated in each instantiation of the law. This is one way out of the trilemma.

Something worth noting about this solution, and on the credit side of its ledger, is that although the fundamental laws of the world come out on this view as absolutely necessary, this necessity is completely *transparent*. It can be seen at once that the cause must bring about its effect. Suppose, instead, that our properties are *not* powers, or do not involve powers. Suppose then that a law of nature, such as a gravitation law, seems to have been discovered. Say it links mass properties and relations of distance together in a certain way. Is this linkage indeed necessary? After all, it is discovered empirically, and the ultimate support for it is based on observation. There is no question of giving a proof of it, as is done in the case of a mathematical theorem. It might be deduced from other laws that we already accept, but that only shifts the problem. The contradictory of the law seems possible. The alleged necessity seems quite untransparent. So is it not contingent? This is not an apodeictic argument, to be sure, but it may seem quite weighty.

All this is altered if the properties essentially involve powers. It even seems analytic or conceptually necessary that a particular instantiating a certain power will, in suitable circumstances, bring about, that is, cause, the manifestation of that power. The particular is a contingent being and so it is possible – if merely possible – that a counterpart particular that lacks that particular power might have existed in the particular's place. (We may or may not be prepared to say that the counterpart is *identical* with the original particular. My present position is that it would not be identical.) But if the manifestation occurs, it occurs with transparent necessity. And even if the law is probabilistic only, the probability of that manifestation is transparently present.

Certain power theorists wish to postulate tropes rather than universals as truthmakers for truths about the (sparse) properties of things (e.g. Martin, 1993, Molnar, 2003 and Heil, 2003). I used to argue that an upholder of tropes is unable to forge the links needed between causes and laws. But that was because I was thinking of the tropes as categorical in nature and not as powers. My reasoning took the following course. Being particulars, tropes cannot be numerically identical in different tokens of what we call 'the same causal sequence' (or other causal connection). Categorical tropes, of course, may resemble each other in greater or lesser degree, right up to exact resemblance. We could then lay down a principle that from resembling causes resembling effects flow. From like causes like effects flow. But, I thought, what truthmaker can we find for this principle? It hardly seems a necessary state of affairs. That the principle should be flouted by actual singular sequences seems not self-contradictory. So here the trilemma seems real. Singular causes can be kept, of course, in a trope theory, but given purely categorical tropes, some Humean-like theory of laws seems inevitable.

If, however, tropes are taken as powers, the 'like causes like' principle can, I now think, be defended rather easily. Powers are defined by their manifestations (or chance of manifestations) in suitable circumstances. These possible manifestations *constitute* the power. Exact resemblance of power-tropes must therefore be exact resemblance in these manifestations. Then the trilemma proves toothless: all three of its propositions can be upheld together. Singular causation can be construed as a relation-trope holding between whatever tropes constitute the token cause and whatever tropes constitute the token effect. Since these tropes are *power*-tropes, the cause will cause the effect of necessity, or else necessitate a certain probability of the effect occurring. These power-tropes will resemble each other, with the limiting case exact resemblance, where classes of tropes closed under exact resemblance are the trope substitute for resemblance. As power-tropes, all the members of the class will make the same contribution to their effects. So a satisfactory substitute is found for the generality that laws ought to exhibit. The trilemma fails.

10.2.2. *Contingent connections between universals to the rescue?*

So both power-universals and power-tropes seem able to evade the trilemma. But we can perhaps get the same sort of result with universals that are *not* powers. Laws of nature, some of us have argued in the past, are not necessary but *contingent* connections between universals. This contingent connection, however, necessitates the corresponding regularity. Furthermore, it, the connection, is *instantiated* in the singular case, just as it is where universals are conceived as powers. If this line can be made good, then again the trilemma is not conclusive.

The idea here is to postulate a causal, or cause-like, connection not merely between particular states of affairs – this billiard ball hitting that billiard ball, and making the latter move – but also, at a higher-order level, between the universals involved in the first-order state of affairs. At the level of particular states of affairs, we do seem to have direct experience of the causal relation, at least in favourable cases (as briefly argued in 10.2, and at greater length in other work). Now consider truths involving general propositions: for instance, <the ingestion of a certain quantity of cyanide causes death>. Current philosophical thought wants to put this in the form of a universally quantified truth about particular events. But this is not its surface form. The surface form asserts a causal connection between *kinds* of events: ingestion of a quantity of cyanide, on the one hand, and death of the one who ingests it, on the other. Its form seems to be: ingestion of cyanide causes death; causes (ingestion of cyanide, death to the ingester). My suggestion is that this is closer to the real form of a causal law. The law *is* a causal connection between these kinds. The same sort of connection which we have direct experience of at the level of particulars is here postulated (on good evidence) to obtain between the kinds themselves. A universally quantified truth can then be *derived* from this truth, analytically it would seem. But the universally quantified truth *by itself* is no more than good evidence for the direct causal connection of the kinds.[2]

It is true that the two kinds involved in my example are very unlikely to be universals. They are second-rate properties. But behind the relatively rough-and-ready classifications that they point to, there will be the true universals (whatever they turn out to be) involved in the situation. The causal connections of these universals will be the ultimate truthmakers involved. It is true, also, that there are certain laws, conservation laws for example, that may seem, superficially, not to be causal laws. But *all* laws involve the instantiation of certain universals *ensuring* that the particular that instantiates them (or some further particular of a certain nature in a certain definite relation to the original particular) instantiates certain further universals. In the case of conservation laws, a system at a certain time and instantiating a certain quantity ensures that at a later time that system, providing there has not been any external interference, instantiates the very same quantity. It seems that we can plausibly postulate that the *ensuring* here is the same ensuring, moved up to a higher level to give a connection of universals, that we have direct experience of in certain cases of perception (pressure on the body and so forth).

---

[2] The best critique of this sort of theory is to be found in van Fraassen's *Laws and Symmetry* (1989, ch. 5). He argues there that there are two problems, the *Identification* problem and the *Inference* problem, each of which can be solved but only at the cost of making the other insoluble. The Identification problem is that of specifying the nature of the connection between the universals involved. I claim that our direct sensory experience of causation allows us to understand the idea that *universals* may be causally connected, and so to understand the claim that arsenic causes death as a causal connection between universals. This, I hope, solves the Identification problem. The Inference problem then seems solved also. For it follows that individual dosings of arsenic will cause individual deaths (or will do so in the absence of countervailing factors). The individual cases of this sort of causation will actually *instantiate* arsenic causing death.

A further notion that may be helpful in understanding this particular so-lution of the problem of the alleged trilemma is that of a *state-of-affairs type*. A schematic example for the monadic case is *something being F*, where F is a universal. Take the simplest case, even if an artificially simple one, where the law is *whatever is F is G* (where G is a further universal). The contingent connection between universals F and G may then be understood as *something's being F* makes it to be the case that *the very same something is G*. The 'makes it to be the case that' is to be understood as 'causing', but here a postulated causing that holds directly between the state-of-affairs types. That constitutes, that *is*, the contingent connection between universals F and G.

The great advantage of thinking in terms of state-of-affairs types comes up when we consider cases where 'like causes like'. If all you say is that a law is a connection of universals, then like causing like appears, absurdly, as a relation of a universal to itself. But if one works with state-of-affairs types, then one can have cases where the type *being the particular that instantiates universal F* brings about the type *some further particular instantiating universal F*.[3] This contingent connection holds in virtue of F plus whatever further universals are needed to spell out, say, the spatial relation holding between the two particulars involved.

We may also notice that an account is needed of *functional* laws, which are, after all, the form of most laws of nature that have a claim to being fundamental. Functional laws stand to the specific nomic connections obtained by substituting particular values for the quantities involved as determinables stand to determinates. This suggests that we should see such laws as linking together genuine determinable properties, ontological determinables, determinables *in re*. In Newtonian physics, the properties of *mass, distance* and *force* are such determinables. Determinates of *mass* and *distance*, determinate masses and distances in a determinate arrangement, generate some determinate gravitational force according to the functional formula. There is, of course, no need to postulate determinable universals as truthmakers for the true application of *every* determinable predicate. *Being coloured* is a determinable, but the science of colour suggests that no universal corresponds to it. (For a spelling out of the argument of this paragraph, see my 1997, 16.1.)

---

[3] Holding as I do a causal theory of identity over time, this allows past temporal parts of particulars to bring about later parts of these particulars, even where the particular is said 'not to change'. Following W. E. Johnson (1964, p. xxi), I call this *immanent* causality as contrasted with *transeunt* causality.

We may, to end this section, notice a further point that is neutral between the various theories that evade the alleged trilemma: singular causation; the law-governed nature of causation; and the generality of laws. Intensionalist theories, whether they postulate a necessary or a contingent connection between the properties involved in cause and effect, do have one very significant advantage over extensionalist theories, where Humean theories are paradigms of extensionalist theories. They make an attack on the problem of induction much easier. It is notorious that extensionalist theories have great difficulty in providing any reason why the unobserved course of events should resemble the observed course. It is no accident that it was Hume who argued for inductive scepticism at the level of reason. But if one is an intensionalist one has 'strong' laws, whether or not they are metaphysically necessary, over and above the mere regularity of the course of nature. One can therefore make an *abductive* inference (inference to the best explanation) from the observed regularities to either powers or laws that *explain* the regularity and predict that it will extend to the unobserved cases. (See Foster, 1983, and my 1991, following on my 1983, in which latter see index under 'induction'.)

10.2.3. *Necessary connections between universals to the rescue?*

Some dislike the account of laws in terms of contingent connections between universals. So we should notice the possibility that the connections between universals involved in laws of nature are necessary rather than contingent. At 4.4 I introduced Donald Baxter's idea that the instantiation of universals is a partial identity, to which I added my own view that the partial identity, granted the notion is intelligible, would have to be accounted as *necessary*. This is because the instantiations of any universal are part of what that universal is. Such partial identity will hold for relations (in particular for external relations) as much as for non-relational properties. (See Armstrong, 2004.) Furthermore, the modal situation would seem to be no different for higher-order relations between universals, which is what I take laws of nature to be. The relation of nomic connection, L (which I take to be best understood as a state-of-affairs type producing a further state-of-affairs type), will have to be partially identical with its universals, schematically F and G. It will then, I think, be a necessary connection, a necessity *in re*. If the types are so connected, then the first-order particulars involved will conform to this linking of types.

10.3. DISPOSITIONS

Some things, I think, have become clearer in the theory of dispositions during the last half-century or so. The first is that where we have the true application of a predicate such as 'brittle' we ought to postulate a property in the object in virtue of which the predicate applies truly. Truthmaker theory leads very naturally to this conclusion. This is not, of course, to say that, even if we accept universals, brittleness is just one property in its different instantiations. Brittleness in one particular may not be the same property in another particular. But where the predicate 'brittle' truly applies to a certain particular, there ought to be a property of that particular to make the application of the predicate true.

The second point, not so often adverted to but I think equally important and widely understood at least at the level of tacit knowledge, is that the concept of a disposition is a *causal* concept. Dispositions are *manifested* from time to time (although a particular particular may never manifest some of its dispositions). The notion of a manifestation is the notion of an empirically possible *effect*, an effect on a disposed object caused by initiating conditions, for instance in the case of brittleness striking or something similar. (The initiating conditions, of course, do their causal work in co-operation with further standing conditions.) So the theory of dispositions is part of the theory of causality. It should be treated as such.

Dispositions are, of course, semantically linked – in some fashion – with conditional propositions, and unmanifested dispositions with counterfactual propositions. A considerable literature now exists on exactly how these propositions should be spelt out, and very sophisticated formulations have been suggested. For our purposes here it will not be necessary to consider these complex formulations. A simple counterfactual such as <if it had been struck, it would have broken> should suffice. Supposing this to be true of a particular glass, we can ask what are its truthmakers, in particular what are its minimal truthmakers. I take it that the postulation of truthmakers called 'counterfactual facts' or 'counterfactual states of affairs' has little appeal. I will also, for obvious naturalist reasons, set aside any using of 'other possible worlds' as truthmakers.

First we need the glass, and a certain amount of its environment. There seems no clear *a priori* answer about just what amount: the situation may differ in different particular cases. (Contemporary physics can at least assure us that the environment to be considered cannot be bigger than the light cone of the glass at the time or times that the counterfactual is supposed true.) If we assume that the simple counterfactual is true, then the truth-maker will be such that it excludes a 'finkish' disposition where the striking would instantaneously cause the glass to lose its brittleness.

A further point is that if the antecedent proposition in the counterfactual is false, as we may assume, then a truthmaker will be required for the negative truth <the glass was not struck>. Such truths have already been discussed in chapter 5. I argued that they have truthmakers, though these are totality states of affairs. But the main truthmaker will be the state of affairs of the glass's having that *property* in virtue of which it is true that if struck, it would have broken. Different philosophers, as we have already noted, conceive of this property in different ways. First, it may be conceived of as a universal or as a particular, a trope. Second, it may be conceived of as a power (in the technical, metaphysical, sense already introduced); or as something categorical, that is, something that is not a power and so does not contain within itself any necessary connection with its potential effect; or, finally, as something that is both categorical and a power (a two-sided view). These are (some of?) the different metaphysical 'fine structures' that may be postulated as constituting the brittleness of the glass. Alas, no simple argument based on the need for truthmakers is going to help with choosing between these different fine structures, something we have already seen in this chapter. The dispute is a matter of choosing between different postulations that all have a claim to be the true truthmakers.

It will be seen that for ontology, in particular for one who sees ontology as a seeking for the right truthmakers, the ontology of dispositions leads back to the fundamental issues involving causes and laws that have already been canvassed in this chapter. Are the properties attributed to objects by dispositional predicates *powers*, with the laws of nature nothing more than these powers? Or is it that the properties themselves are not powers, and the laws of nature are a matter of contingent (or perhaps necessary) relations holding between the properties or, in the Humean version, a matter of contingent regularities in the instantiation of these properties?

10.4. AGAINST POWER THEORIES OF PROPERTIES

At this point, though, I will explain why, despite the attractions of the power view of properties, I am nevertheless a categoricalist about properties. (See also Armstrong, 1999a.) The great difficulty that I see is that not *all* properties, not even all scientifically respectable properties, sparse properties in Lewis's phrase, can plausibly be treated as powers. (When I say 'all properties' here I understand the phrase in the sense that includes relations.) Here is the argument. Suppose that the world consists of particulars having properties in the narrow sense and related to each other by external relations. (Internal relations may, I trust, be ignored as not constituting any ontological addition. The truthmakers for such relations are just the terms of the relation.) Now suppose that these properties and relations are nothing but powers. It will follow that the manifestations of these powers, when they occur, can themselves be nothing but cases of particulars coming to have certain powers. After all, manifestations are nothing but certain particulars coming to have certain properties, and on the theory being criticized all properties dissolve into powers. But could there be a world of this sort? Powers must surely issue in manifestations that are something more than just powers. A world where potency never issued in act, but only in more potency, would be one where one travelled without ever having the possibility of arriving.

It is important to be clear that this argument will, by itself, catch only what one might call a Power Maximalist, one who makes every property a power, and nothing but a power. Among actual power theorists it catches, as far as I know, only one theorist: Sydney Shoemaker. In a debate with Richard Swinburne, Shoemaker outlines his power theory of properties and explicitly says that his account 'could be extended to cover relations as well as properties' (Shoemaker 1980, p. 296). In his reply Swinburne raises the objection of the previous paragraph (Swinburne 1980). Shoemaker has since given up this position (see his 1998), but I have not been able to understand what his new account of property-powers is.

The objection to Power Maximalism has been well understood by various other power theorists, for instance Brian Ellis and George Molnar (Ellis, 1999 and 2001, 3.12; Molnar, 2003, ch. 10: 'Non-powers'). What they do is to walk away from Power *Maximalism*. They exempt certain properties. Thus Ellis concedes that 'spatial, temporal, and other primary properties and relationships are not causal powers' (Ellis, 1999, p. 42).[4] Molnar exempts external relations, in particular spatiotemporal relations such as distance. Let us here concede, for the sake of argument at least, that these concessions will give enough to form a coherent conception of what the particulars are in themselves over and above their powers to affect

---

[4] In a recent verbal communication Ellis has confined these properties and relations to the spatiotemporal ones.

other particulars. One relation that will have to be categorical is causation itself, because it is essentially involved in the manifestations of powers.

These properties that are not powers I call categorical properties. (Molnar simply calls them non-powers.) A dilemma can be put. Are these non-powers epiphenomenal? If they are, then it is very difficult to see, for a naturalist at least, how we can have any cognizance of them. If they do not have causal efficacy, or any nomic link to other properties, any link that causally or nomically differentiates one of these properties or relations from others, they will be completely unknown to us. Yet, of course, we are well acquainted with such relations as distance, and difference in distances.

Let us consider two particulars, each having some mass, which attract each other according to some formula, say the Newtonian inverse square law. The masses we think of as powers, but the distances are non-powers, given the theory we are examining. But the forces generated between the two particulars vary inversely with the square of the distance. Have not the two particulars got to 'know', as it were, at what distance they are from each other if they are to exert the right amount of force on each other? Struggling with this difficulty, Molnar speaks of the mass-properties that are powers being 'sensitive' to the distance. But to be sensitive to something is to be able to pick up signals from it. Sensitivity is dispositional/causal *in its essence*. For the particular case this means that Molnar is conceding that distance actually has some sort of causal efficacy. So for him causal efficacy is not confined to powers. And that causal efficacy will presumably be contingent, not necessary. (And if it is necessary, it cannot be a *transparent* necessity.) So for Molnar and Ellis it seems that there will be an element of contingency in the Newtonian gravitation law.

The situation is perhaps even a bit worse than this. Just as the conjunction of a contingent truth and a necessary truth is a contingent truth, so a causal law that involves co-operating powers and non-powers in the cause will be a contingent law. Such causes will yield different effects 'in different possible worlds'. What account should a power-theorist give of such laws? Not, one would trust, a regularity account! The obvious thing to do, it seems to me, is to adopt the alternative 'strong law' account of laws and construe the contribution of non-powers to the laws of nature as being relations between universals. How in detail this is to be worked out, I do not venture to say.

At this point I think that we begin to see the attractions of C. B. Martin's view that a power account should nevertheless do justice to what Martin thinks of as the *qualitative* side of properties. (Remembering, of course, that properties are tropes for him.) As his view was originally articulated properties had two 'sides', the qualitative and the power side (Armstrong, Martin and Place, 1996, see index under 'Limit view'). The problem for him, then, was to say how the two sides relate to each other. Is it a contingent or a necessary connection? There are difficulties for both hypotheses. Contingent connection would require a whole extra set of contingent correlation laws. But if the connection is necessary then the trouble again is that the necessity, unlike the necessity found in the operation of the powers or the necessities found in logic and mathematics, is a *completely untransparent* necessity. Why are this quality and this power linked necessarily together? No answer seems forthcoming.

More recently Martin has suggested that what we have in the 'two' sides is really *identity* (Martin 1997, sec. 12). He has been followed in this by John Heil (2003, ch. 11), who suggests Necker's cube as model. Heil speaks of this as an identity theory, and explicitly draws a parallel with the identity theory of mind, once regarded by many as a very paradoxical theory. This parallel overlooks the point that the identity theory of mind *was* genuinely paradoxical until Smart put forward the thesis that mental ascriptions involve something topic-neutral. In doing so he pointed to a conceptual gap that materialists could hope to plug with purely physical descriptions of what goes on in the brain. The topic-neutral thesis then remained itself controversial, but it was easy to see that if topic-neutrality were once accepted, the identity of the mental and the physical was straightforward enough and, true or false, not particularly puzzling. No such demystification is offered in the case of the new identity theory, although it cries out for such treatment. The attraction of Necker's cube is presumably this: as the cube 'changes' it still suggests 'the very same object' to the perceiver. The only change is that the object appears differently related to the perceiver. But the change is very small, while the apparent difference between qualities (with their just-there-ness) and powers (with their pointing to their possible manifestations) is immense. As well identify a raven with a writing desk. I think the two-sided view, with all its difficulties, was better than this.

These are my main reasons for not going along with the way of powers. I believe, nevertheless, that Martin's approach is on the right track. We do need a two-sided approach to properties. Let me put it in this way. Properties are not powers. But properties *have* powers. They bestow powers. (If they did not, we could know nothing about them.) But these powers are not to be conceived of in the way that Martin and most other necessitarians about causality conceive them. They spring instead from the connections between universals that constitute the laws of nature. We could call this approach a 'soft' theory of powers. It does not deny the truth <the properties of objects bestow powers upon them>. That is accepted as a truth. But it offers a different truthmaker for these powers: the way that the intrinsic properties of things are nomically linked to further properties in the thing or in its environment.

There is scope here for what may be called, following Lewis, a *causal role* account of basic physical concepts. Mass, to take that as our example, can certainly and with advantage be *defined* as that monadic property (or class of properties, to allow for different quantities of mass) which bestows certain powers (soft sense) on those objects that have mass, details to be spelt out by physics.

10.5. THE ATTRACTION OF POWER THEORIES EXPLAINED AWAY

I think it must be conceded that the power view is the most elegant resolution of the truthmaker question here. It is only because, in my view, this success is outweighed by difficulties elsewhere (the problem of properties that are not powers, or the problem of identifying the qualitative and the power side of properties) that I reject it. In postulating truthmakers there are trade-offs to be made. Economy and elegance may be present at one point, and absent at another. So let us consider what a 'laws of nature' as opposed to a power view should say about dispositions at the time that they are not being manifested. I think that the upholder of the laws of nature view can, to a degree, explain the attraction of the power view even if the power view is false.

Given an account that appeals to laws rather than powers, an unmanifested disposition is a property of the disposed thing, a property that is really there, but it is a mere part of the conditions that are required for manifestation. (An initiating, triggering cause is lacking.) On a power view, however, the property of its own essence is that which, in conjunction with other powers, and perhaps certain categorical, non-power, properties, points to a certain manifestation. That is why it is *transparent* that it is necessary that the power should, with the right assistance, manifest itself in this way. Now, even if the power view is not true, there may be important *biological* reasons, reasons important for the conduct of life, in thinking of dispositions as powers. It may be a good *picture* to have. (Compare the possible worlds.)

Many of the things in life offer threats and promises. But very often these threats and promises can only be carried out provided something else is added, *an addition that we can do something about*. If we 'do the right thing' the threat will not be executed, or the promise will be fulfilled. But we need to take care. Often threat and promise are found in the very same thing. The sharp knife will cut things that need to be cut admirably, and so it is useful, but it has to be handled with care lest it cut something we do not want to be cut, such as our flesh. Under these circumstances, it will help in negotiating our way among the unmanifested dispositions of things if we tend to think of them as actually pointing to these manifestations in the way that powers do. If in imagination we credit things with powers *in the ontological sense*, if we see the potential cutting in the knife, the potential death in the poison, this may school our thoughts, easily influenced by our imagination, in avoiding dangers and pursuing opportunities.

None of this is any direct argument against a metaphysic of powers, of course. An upholder of that ontology could perfectly well accept the point just made. But suppose, as I think, that the powers ontology is, on balance, less satisfactory than a laws of nature ontology. Then some (not all) of the attractions of the powers view can be explained away. To be able plausibly to explain certain attractions in the view of one's opponent is a strengthening of one's position.

10.6. WHAT SORT OF TERMS DOES THE CAUSAL RELATION TAKE?

This section, the last in the chapter, is not closely connected with the earlier sections. But it seems an important point to notice. It is customary to say that causation holds between *events*, and I have gone along with that earlier in this chapter. If we are looking for truthmakers, though, we need to take care. Events, as they are ordinarily conceived, regularly involve not only comings to be, but also passings away. A billiard ball hits another such ball. It was originally not in contact with a second ball, but comes to be in contact, a contact involving acting upon the second one. It originally lacked a certain relational property (the contact), but acquires that property. This may be said to be the cause. The second ball was not originally in motion, but comes to be in motion. This may be said to be the effect. *Prima facie*, negative properties are involved.

We, however, have set our faces against negative properties (ch. 5), one of the reasons, indeed, being that negative properties would not bestow any causal power. We have not denied negative truths. It is true that, at the beginning, the first ball lacked contact with the second ball. But as truthmaker for this truth we have suggested a *general* state of affairs: each member of the totality of the relevant properties of the first ball (at the beginning) is different from the property of being in contact with the second ball. If, in addition, we think of causality as 'the cement of the universe', the central relation that lawfully binds things together in the world, we will not be very impressed by these general states of affairs as terms of the causal relation. We will want the cause to be something *positive* – a particular's having some positive property – and equally we will want the effect to be something – again a particular's having some positive property. This suggests that the ontological terms of the causal relation should be restricted to states of affairs, events in a somewhat restricted sense.

11

Time

It always seems valuable in metaphysics to consider what the truthmakers are for any proposition held to be true. Sometimes, however, this will not do a great deal more than clarify the issues involved. Perhaps this is the case in questions about the nature of causality and law, considered in the last chapter. In other cases, however, insisting on considering what the truthmakers are will actually help to push the discussion in some particular direction. This seems evident in the case of counterfactual truths. It also seems plausible in the case of certain questions about the metaphysics of time.

Here are three positions. First: only the present exists. This view now bears the name Presentism. Second: all that exists is the past, up to the present moment. We might call this Pastism (another unlovely term to which I see no satisfactory alternative). Third: past, present and future all exist. This is the Omnitemporal view. Once we accept the demand for truthmakers, then, I suggest, there is a strong *prima facie* case for accepting the Omnitemporal view.

Surely there are truths about the past. It is true, and known to be true, that Julius Caesar was assassinated by Brutus, Cassius and others in 44 BC on the Ides of March. Only a very extreme sceptic could call this truth into question. And any upholder of truthmakers will demand truthmakers for this truth. That there are truthmakers for truths about the present presumably all parties will grant, if they allow truthmakers at all.

That there are truths about the future is perhaps a little more controversial, but not, I think, seriously so. 'What's to come is still unsure', Shakespeare's song tells us. Unsure perhaps, but that is an epistemological matter. There can be truth without knowledge. Suppose that in the year 2003 (as it is of this writing) I assert that the sun will rise as usual during 2004. It is likely enough that this, and many, many other statements now made about the future are true. Truthmakers are required for these truths. The Omnitemporal view provides straightforward truthmakers for all truths about the past and the future. The past exists. The future exists. They are 'there' (they exist, they are real) to be truthmakers.

We consider the Presentist first.[1] What is this theory to say about Julius Caesar? The Presentist will say that Caesar did exist, but (unless he is an immortal soul) he no longer exists. These are indeed acceptable ways of speaking, and that they are acceptable is an important part of the case for Presentism. But if truthmaker theory is accepted along with Presentism, what truthmaker can be provided for the truth <Caesar existed>? The obvious truthmaker, at least, is Caesar himself. But to allow Caesar as a truthmaker seems to allow reality to the past, contrary to the hypothesis.

There seem to be three lines of defence available to the Presentist. The first is to postulate truthmakers for truths about the past and the present *in the present*. The second is to find truthmakers *outside time*. The third is to accept *non-existents* as truthmakers, provided that they existed or will exist.

If the Presentist opts for truthmakers in the present then the best way to proceed seems to postulate *properties*, constantly changing indexical properties that attach to the ever-changing present. The truthmaker for <Julius Caesar does not exist but did exist> will be a property of the present. That property will be like a determinable, and falling under this 'determinable' will be the determinate property of existing just so long ago as 44 BC. Similar things will have to be said about the future, what does not exist but will exist. These too are properties of the present, the only real thing in the natural world.

But Keller points to a serious problem for these alleged properties. Are they to be taken to be *relational* or *non-relational* properties of the really existing present? On the face of it, they ought to be relational properties. The property of *Caesar's having existed* ought, it seems, to involve a relation to the man himself. But nothing exists to have this relation to, if *existed* necessitates *does not exist*. A Meinongian theory that allows non-existents into one's ontology, or a theory which distinguishes between existence and subsistence, would seem to be the only options here.

Keller himself advocates treating the properties as non-relational (intrinsic) properties of the present. But this monstrous piling of extra properties upon the present seems unsatisfactory. The Caesarian property has somehow to be attached to the (non-existent) *Caesar*. It must somehow point

---

[1] I am indebted here to an unpublished paper by Simon Keller, 'How to be a Presentist'. See also Tooley, 1997, 8.6.

to Caesar, but how is that to be done? Perhaps it could be the proposition <Caesar existed>, construed as a property of the present. But the proposition still needs a truthmaker. What can that truthmaker be?

At this point one could consider the second line of defence and postulate a realm of truths about the past and present that exist outside time. This will at least avoid a changing set of properties accompanying the continually changing present. But the truths will still lack truthmakers. Indeed, such a realm of truths seems to be disturbingly like the Omnitemporal view because it models space-time (along with anything else that is thought to exist). Space-time is traded in for an abstract entity, in the philosopher's contemporary or Quinean sense of 'abstract'. The Omnitemporal account is a lot simpler!

This brings us to the third line of defence of Presentism, one suggested to me by John Heil. It seems the best available, though it is still very radical. It is a proposal, in effect, to modify truthmaking theory. It relies on the point that though Caesar does not exist, yet unlike Jove, he exist*ed*. It then urges that although <Caesar exists> lacks a truthmaker, and is not true, yet that proposition was once true and *did* have a truthmaker. That, it is then suggested, is all we need demand: that the proposition have a truthmaker *at some time*.

I find such a re-doing of truthmaker theory very painful and artificial. But it also faces, I think, an internal problem. What of the proposition <this proposition *was* true>? It must certainly be accounted a true proposition by a Presentist. What is its truthmaker? It would seem that it does not have one, because there is nothing in the present in virtue of which it is true. Indeed, consider the proposition <there has been a past>. That is true. Russellian fantasies of the world starting a moment ago, and so there only seeming to have been a past, are certainly false. But what can the proposition's truthmaker be? And to exempt such propositions from the need to have truthmakers is to restrict the scope of truthmaker theory in an extraordinary way.

This leads on to another point that, if good, will be an objection to each of the ways that a Presentist might try to come to terms with truthmaker theory. This concerns truths where a relation is asserted to hold between the present, on the one hand, and past and future, on the other. <Caesar's death in 44 BC is before the present time at which I type these words> is a truth. What are we to say about its truthmaker? It is a strange state of affairs: an external relation holding between a non-existent and an existent. Can we admit such relations? They are very ugly additions to an ontology!

The Omnitemporal view, however, does have to face at least one question. If the past is real, why is it that we say, and say with truth, that Caesar no longer exists? But this question seems easy to answer. The Omnitemporalist will urge that there are two senses of the word 'exists' involved. It may mean 'exists now', and in that sense Caesar does not exist. But it may mean 'is a reality', and Caesar is, of course, a reality (in the way that Jove is not). The second sense is the ontological sense. That 'exists' sometimes means 'exists now', the Omnitemporalist will say, does no more than bear witness to the central importance of the present moment to us, considered as animals that have to make their way in the world.

This argument, and this little bit of pragmatic semantics, is not of course decisive, even if we have embraced truthmakers. It is worth noticing, then, that there are two further arguments against Presentism that can be added to considerations drawn from considering the question of truthmakers. The first of these arguments is well known. It is the difficulty that Special Relativity treats the present as a relative notion. That two events occur simultaneously is held to be a relative matter in that theory, relative to the velocity of frames of reference. No absolute simultaneity is admitted. So whether events A and B both exist would, given Presentism, receive different answers relative to different frames. This is also a difficulty for Pastism.

A further problem that can be added arises concerning the extent of the present. In ordinary language what we account 'the present' expands and contracts to suit our convenience. But given any continuous period of time, if we can distinguish either immediately, or as the result of scientific measurement, a before from an after, then for the Presentist this span embraces non-being as well as being. The metaphysical present will be a strict instant, or, if time is not infinitely divisible, the present will be a minimum granule of duration. But strict instants or minimum granules of duration, if these exist, cannot be experienced. Contemporary psychology shows that temporal discriminations, the *just noticeable differences* with respect to duration, are far coarser than that. The metaphysical present thus becomes a theoretical entity. 'Exists now', taken as what really exists, is never actually experienced. This is ironic when it is considered that it is the *experience* of the present, Iago's 'even now, very now . . . ', that helps to fuel the conviction of Presentists.

This second additional difficulty does not arise for Pastism. The world, the whole of being, is on this view an object that is continually being added to along the temporal dimension. The past exists, the present in the strictest, narrowest sense exists, but is no more than the growing temporal edge or limit of being. The truthmaker for its being *now* is the whole of the temporal dimension of what exists. It is only the future that does not exist. We are, of course, much more reliably informed about the past than we are about the future. According to the Pastist, this epistemological fact is correlated with, and reflects, the ontological situation – what's to come does not even exist yet. This seems to me a much more attractive view than Presentism.

Nevertheless, the demand for truthmakers for truths about the future seems to make about as much trouble for Pastism as it makes for Presentism. It seems clear that even if we do not know much about the future, still we can have true beliefs, and make true statements about, the future. What is their truthmaker? Pastism is defended by Michael Tooley in his *Time, Tense and Causation* (1997), already referred to. (It was also the view of C. D. Broad.) In chapter 10 Tooley confronts objections to his 'dynamic' view, as he calls it, but does not explicitly confront the objection from truthmakers. It does appear, though, that he would need to distinguish between a truth solely about the future having an actual truthmaker (false) and its coming to have a truthmaker in the future (true).[2] In his discussion, already referred to, of Presentism at 8.6, however, he argues *against* such a view as applied to the *past*, and makes explicit appeal to the need for truthmakers. On pages 233–4 he considers a Presentist who argues that the statement 'there are dinosaurs' *was* true. He says that the Presentist can only interpret this as asserting that there is a past time at which the sentence is true, but then argues at some length that the Presentist is unable to provide truthmakers for the truth that there is a past time. But in the same way, how can the Pastist such as himself make sense of the truth that there is future time?

We may note that Tooley also has to deal with the objection from Special Relativity. He devotes chapter 11 to this, propounding an ingenious theory that he argues will both uphold the idea of an absolute present, and yet not be an ad hoc addition to our current physics. I do not have the expertise to assess this.

---

[2] I infer this from his emphasizing a distinction between 'the concept of being actual *simpliciter*, and the concept of being actual as of a time' (1997, p. 305). Such a view of being argues a parallel view of truth.

There are, of course, all sorts of problems concerning the metaphysics of time. It is my impression, however, that these problems will largely be solved *within* the natural sciences. It will be physics and cosmology that tell us the true nature of time. It is, perhaps, only in the philosophical disputes between Presentism, Pastism and the Omnitemporal view that truthmaker theory seems to favour the Omnitemporal view by indicating problems for the other two positions.

References

Anscombe, G. E. M. 1975. 'Causality and determination'. In *Causation and Conditionals*, ed. Ernest Sosa. Oxford Readings in Philosophy. Oxford: Oxford University Press.

Aristotle. 1941. *The Basic Works of Aristotle*, ed. Richard McKeon. New York: Random House.

Armstrong, D. M. 1978. *A Theory of Universals*. Cambridge: Cambridge University Press.

1983. *What is a Law of Nature?* Cambridge: Cambridge University Press.

1989a. *A Combinatorial Theory of Possibility*. Cambridge: Cambridge University Press.

1989b. *Universals: An Opinionated Introduction*. Boulder, Colo.: Westview Press.

1991. 'What makes induction rational?' *Dialogue* (Canada), 30: 503–11.

1997. *A World of States of Affairs*. Cambridge: Cambridge University Press.

1999a. 'The causal theory of properties: properties according to Shoemaker, Ellis, and others'. *Philosophical Topics*, 26: 25–37.

1999b. 'A naturalist program: epistemology and ontology'. *Proceedings and Addresses of the American Philosophical Association*, 73.2: 77–89.

2004. 'How do particulars stand to universals?' In *Oxford Studies in Metaphysics*, vol. 1, ed. Dean Zimmerman, 139–154.

Armstrong, D. M., Martin, C. B. and Place, U. T. 1996. *Dispositions: A Debate*, ed. Tim Crane. London: Routledge.

Baxter, Donald. 2001. 'Instantiation as partial identity'. *Australasian Journal of Philosophy*, 79: 449–64.

Bergmann, Gustav. 1967. *Realism: A Critique of Brentano and Meinong*. Madison: University of Wisconsin Press.

1992. *New Foundations of Ontology*, ed. W. Heald. Madison: University of Wisconsin Press.

Bigelow, John. 1988. *The Reality of Numbers*. Oxford: Clarendon Press.

Campbell, Keith. 1990. *Abstract Particulars*. Oxford: Basil Blackwell.

Cox, Damian. 1997. 'The trouble with truth-makers'. *Pacific Philosophical Quarterly*, 78: 45–62.

Davidson, Donald. 1995. 'Law and cause'. *Dialectica*, 49: 265–79.

Demos, Raphael. 1917. 'A discussion of certain types of negative propositions'. *Mind*, 26: 188–96.

Dowe, Phil. 2000. *Physical Causation*. New York: Cambridge University Press.

References

Ellis, Brian. 1999. 'Response to David Armstrong'. In *Causation and Laws of Nature*, ed. Howard Sankey. Dordrecht: Kluwer Academic Publishers, 39–43.

——— 2001. *Scientific Essentialism*. Cambridge: Cambridge University Press.

Fales, Evan. 1990. *Causation and Universals*. London: Routledge.

Forrest, Peter and Armstrong, D. M. 1987. 'The nature of number'. *Philosophical Papers*, 16: 165–86.

Forrest, Peter and Khlentzos, Drew. 2000, eds. *Truth Maker and Its Variants*. Special issue of *Logique et Analyse*, nos. 169–70.

Foster, John. 1983. 'Induction, explanation and natural necessity'. *Proceedings of the Aristotelian Society*, 83: 87–101.

Gigerenzer, Gerd. 2002. *Reckoning with Risk*. London: Allen Lane, The Penguin Press. (Published in the USA as *Calculated Risk*.)

Hager, Paul. 1994. *Continuity and Change in the Development of Russell's Philosophy*. Dordrecht: Kluwer Academic Publishers.

Hamming, R. W. 1980. 'The unreasonable effectiveness of mathematics'. *American Mathematical Monthly*, 87.2.

Hegel, G. W. F. 1956 [1840]. *The Philosophy of History*, trans. J. Sibree. New York: Dover.

Heil, John. 2003. *From an Ontological Point of View*. New York: Oxford University Press.

Hellman, Geoffrey. 1989. *Mathematics without Numbers: Towards a Modal-Structural Interpretation*. Oxford: Clarendon Press.

Hochberg, Herbert. 1984. 'Universals, particulars, and predication'. *Logic, Ontology, and Language*, 263–78. Munich: Philosophia Verlag.

——— 1999. *Complexes and Consciousness*. Stockholm: Thales.

——— 2001. *The Positivist and the Ontologist: Bergmann, Carnap and Logical Realism*. Amsterdam: Editions Rodopi.

Holton, Richard. 1999. 'Dispositions all the way round'. *Analysis*, 59: 9–14.

Horwich, Paul. 1990. *Truth*. Oxford: Basil Blackwell.

——— Forthcoming. 'Une critique de la théorie des vérifacteurs'. In *La Structure du Monde: Objets, Propriétés, État de Choses*, ed. Jean-Maurice Monnoyer. Paris: Vrin.

Hume, David. 1960 [1739]. *A Treatise of Human Nature*, ed. L. A. Selby-Bigge. Oxford: Clarendon Press.

Johnson, W. E. 1964 [1924]. *Logic*, Part III. New York: Dover.

Kanigel, Robert. 1992. *The Man who Knew Infinity*. London: Abacus.

Kirkham, Richard L. 1992. *Theories of Truth: A Critical Introduction*. Cambridge, Mass.: MIT Press/Bradford Books.

Lewis, David. 1986. *On the Plurality of Worlds*. Oxford: Basil Blackwell.

——— 1991. *Parts of Classes*. Oxford: Basil Blackwell.

——— 2001. 'Truth-making and difference-making'. *Noûs*, 35: 602–15.

——— 2004. 'Void and object'. In *Causation and Counterfactuals*, ed. John Collins, Ned Hall and L. A. Paul, ch. 10. Cambridge, Mass.: MIT Press.

Lycan, William G. 2001. 'Moore against the new skeptics'. *Philosophical Studies*, 103: 35–53.

Martin, C. B. 1993. 'Power for realists'. In *Ontology, Causality and Mind*, ed. John Bacon, Keith Campbell and Lloyd Reinhardt, 175–94. Cambridge: Cambridge University Press.

1996. 'How it is: entities, absences and voids'. *Australasian Journal of Philosophy*, 74: 57–65.

1997. 'On the need for properties: the road to Pythagoreanism and back'. *Synthèse*, 112: 193–231.

Molnar, George. 2000. 'Truthmakers for negative truths'. *Australasian Journal of Philosophy*, 78: 72–86.

2003. *Powers*, ed. Stephen Mumford. Oxford: Oxford University Press.

Mulligan, Kevin, Simons, Peter and Smith, Barry. 1984. 'Truth-makers'. *Philosophy and Phenomenological Research*, 44: 287–321.

Plantinga, Alvin. 1974. *The Nature of Necessity*. Oxford: Clarendon Press.

Plato. 1961. *The Collected Dialogues*, ed. Edith Hamilton and Huntingdon Cairns. New York: Bolligen Foundation.

Putnam, Hilary. 1975. 'Mathematics without foundations'. *Philosophical Papers*, vol. 1. Cambridge: Cambridge University Press.

Quine, W. V. 1966. *The Ways of Paradox and Other Essays*. New York: Random House.

Read, Stephen. 2000. 'Truthmakers and the disjunction thesis'. *Mind*, 109: 67–79.

Restall, Greg. 1995. 'What truthmakers can do for you'. Automated Reasoning Project, Australian National University, Canberra.

1996. 'Truthmakers, entailment and necessity'. *Australasian Journal of Philosophy*, 74: 331–40.

Rodriguez-Pereyra, Gonzalo. 1997. 'There might be nothing: the subtraction argument improved'. *Analysis*, 57: 159–66.

2002. *Resemblance Nominalism: A Solution to the Problem of Universals*. Oxford: Oxford University Press.

Rosen, Gideon. 1995. 'Armstrong on classes as states of affairs'. *Australasian Journal of Philosophy*, 73: 613–25.

Russell, Bertrand. 1940. *An Inquiry into Meaning and Truth*. London: George Allen and Unwin.

1948. *Human Knowledge: Its Scope and Limits*. London: George Allen and Unwin.

1959. *My Philosophical Development*. London: George Allen and Unwin.

1972 [1918]. *Russell's Logical Atomism*, ed. David Pears. London: Fontana.

Russell, Bertrand, and Whitehead, Alfred North. *Principia Mathematica*, vol. 1, 2nd edn. Cambridge: Cambridge University Press.

Ryle, Gilbert. 1949. *The Concept of Mind*. London: Hutchinson, 1949.

Shapiro, Stewart. 1997. *Philosophy of Mathematics: Structure and Ontology*. New York: Oxford University Press.

Shoemaker, Sydney. 1980. 'Properties, causation and projectibility'. In *Applications of Inductive Logic*, ed. L. J. Cohen and Mary Hesse. Oxford: Oxford University Press.

1984. 'Causality and properties'. *Identity, Cause and Mind: Philosophical Essays*. Cambridge: Cambridge University Press.

1998. 'Causal and metaphysical necessity'. *Pacific Philosophical Quarterly*, 79: 59–77.

Simons, Peter. 1994. 'Particulars in particular clothing: three trope theories of substance'. *Philosophy and Phenomenological Research*, 54: 553–75.

Sorensen, Roy. 2001. *Vagueness and Contradiction*. Oxford: Clarendon Press.

Swinburne, Richard. 1980. 'Properties, causation and projectibility: reply to Shoemaker'. In *Applications of Inductive Logic*, ed. L. J. Cohen and Mary Hesse. Oxford: Oxford University Press.

Tooley, Michael. 1997. *Time, Tense, and Causation*. Oxford: Oxford University Press.

Twain, Mark, 1962 [1883]. *Life on the Mississippi*. Oxford: Oxford University Press.

van Fraassen, Bas C. 1989. *Laws and Symmetry*. Oxford: Clarendon Press.

van Inwagen, Peter. 1996. 'It is wrong, everywhere, always, and for anyone, to believe anything upon insufficient evidence'. In *Faith, Freedom and Rationality*, ed. Jeff Jordan and Daniel Howard. Rowman and Littlefield.

Wigner, Eugene. 1960. 'The unreasonable effectiveness of mathematics in the natural sciences'. Communication in *Pure and Applied Mathematics*, 13.1: 1–14.

Williams, Donald C. 1966. *Principles of Empirical Realism*. Springfield, Ill.: Charles C. Thomas.

Williams, Michael. 2002. 'On some critics of deflationism'. In *What is Truth?* ed. Richard Schantz, 146–58. Berlin: Walter de Gruyter.

Wittgenstein, Ludwig. 1961 [1921]. *Tractatus Logico-Philosophicus*, trans. D. F. Pears and B. F. McGuinness. London: Routledge and Kegan Paul.

Index